THE ART OF TIME

MICHAEL KIRBY, a sculptor and theatre artist, is an assistant professor at Saint Francis College in Brooklyn, New York. He is the author of *Happenings* (1965), and until recently he was a contributing editor of *The Drama Review*.

THE ART of TIME

Essays on the Avant-Garde

by Michael Kirby

E. P. DUTTON & CO., INC., NEW YORK, 1969

V

Published simultaneously in Canada by
Clarke, Irwin & Company Limited, Toronto and Vancouver

Library of Congress Catalog Card Number: 69-17222

"The New Theatre" is reprinted from *Tulane Drama Review*, Vol. 10, No. 2, Winter 1965.

"The Uses of Film in the New Theatre" is reprinted from *Tulane Drama Review*, Vol. 11, No. 1, Fall 1966.

"*Calling*" (in "The Activity: A New Art Form") is reprinted from *Tulane Drama Review*, Vol. 10, No. 2, Winter 1965.

"*The First and Second Wilderness*" (in "Performance Chronology") is reprinted from *Tulane Drama Review*, Vol. 10, No. 2, Winter 1965.

"*Room 706*" (in "Performance Chronology") is reprinted from *The Drama Review*, Vol. 12, No. 3, Spring 1968.

"Sculpture as a Visual Instrument" is reprinted from *Art International*.

"The Experience of Kinesis" is reprinted from *Art News*, Vol. 66, No. 10, February 1968.

The epigraph from *The Seven Ages of the Theatre* by Richard Southern is used with the permission of the publishers, Hill and Wang, Inc.

The quotation from *Eye and Brain: The Psychology of Seeing* by R. L. Gregory is used with the permission of the publishers, The McGraw-Hill Book Company. Copyright © 1966 by R. L. Gregory.

The quotations from *Subcortical Mechanisms of Behavior: The Psychological Functions of Primitive Parts* by Robert A. McCleary and Robert Y. Moore is used with the permission of the publishers, Basic Books, Inc.

The quotation from *The Influence of Culture on Visual Perception* by Marshall H. Segall, Donald T. Campbell, and Melville J. Herskovits is used with the permission of the publishers, The Bobbs-Merrill Company, Inc. Copyright © 1966 by The Bobbs-Merrill Company, Inc.

To E. M. K.

Contents

So we are forced again to
a strange conclusion about
early theatre. Just as it
did not matter whether you
heard all the words of a
show so also it did not
matter whether you saw
all of the action.

RICHARD SOUTHERN
in *The Seven Ages of the
Theatre*

Preface

This book was not written or conceived as a complete entity. Many of the essays were first published elsewhere; they were never intended to lead into or to explain each other. The new material that I have written particularly for the book also tends to be self-sufficient, and no attempt has been made to survey the *avant-garde* in its entirety or to discuss all of its aspects.

And yet I think that this is not merely a collection of essays. Except for the brief stories that I have included because they seemed to explain things that could be explained in no other way, there is an intentional impersonality in the writing style. I do not state explicitly what I have felt was good or bad about particular works. You will find no interpretations, either emotional or sociopolitical. I am not a critic. I merely try to describe, explain, define, and categorize. But if the style and approach tend to be impersonal, the unity of the book itself is a result of its entirely personal basic character and nature.

I do not think of myself as a writer, and I write only when something seems particularly important and the opportunity arises. (In this context, I should like to thank Richard Schechner for asking me to write several of these essays, which first appeared in the *Tulane Drama Review* and *The Drama Review*.) But, especially when you write only about things that are inescapable, so to speak, the value judgments that I have denied making will still be implicitly present and obvious. It will probably be much more apparent to you than it is to me that this is a biased and slanted book. It is here that its unity and cohesiveness will be clearest.

For this reason, I have not hesitated to describe my own work in sculpture, which has taken the majority of my time and thought for the last decade, and in performance. The juxtaposition of these descriptions with my writings on the sculpture and performances of other artists may make certain things apparent that I could not put into words. The somewhat diverse types of writing in this book mirror the diverse activities of my life, but, as with life, there is a unity and cohesiveness that is more than the sum of the various elements.

The unity, then, is not necessarily an intellectual one. I am not going to introduce each of the essays and try to justify its place in the whole. And no attempt has been made to rewrite completely those essays that were previously published, although certain details have been changed. (In this connection, I will point out that *The new theatre* essay uses the phrase uncapitalized, while it is capitalized in *The Uses of Film in the New Theatre*. I have chosen to let this inconsistency stand. After the former essay appeared in *TDR*, *The New York Times* printed a long reactionary letter attacking "the New Theatre." I had not used capitals because there have already been many new theatres and they will continue to develop, but after reading the letter I was impressed by the capitalization and employed it in the later "continuation." In my usage, the phrase applied to alogical performances. Now, with capitals, it is being applied to something entirely different: the Grotowski-oriented Off Off-Broadway emphasis on physical movement.)

An intellectual unity to the book is provided, of course, by the long essay on the aesthetics of the avant-garde that opens the collection. All of the works discussed later, or at least the manner in which they are discussed, may be related to the theoretical concepts put forward there. One common denominator of these works can be seen in contrast to what could be called "Greenbergian" criticism. Clement Greenberg has proposed that each art form has historically refined its goals to the point where each attempts to do only what it alone can do. Thus, to oversimplify, that painting is best that does only those things that are unique to painting. Although this school of criticism is very important and I admire much of its writing, I cannot accept the basic premise. The so-called forms of art are merely intellectual constructs that are helpful in describing experience. They do not limit it. We cannot reject things merely because they do not fit into a category. Nor do categories necessarily determine values, although Greenberg's criticism has influenced many artists and therefore is of great worth even though it is not fundamentally correct.

If the criticism of art did depend upon art forms, many of the works described in this book would be beyond criticism, or would be rejected summarily as "bad," merely because they were outside of a traditional form. While Greenberg sees history as purifying forms, I see it as breaking down the autonomy of formal definitions. One of the strongest tendencies in avant-garde art has been toward what Dick Higgins has called "intermedia"—art that exists between prevalent definitions or makes use of materials and concepts from two different disciplines. (I shall not go so far, however, as to say that a work is good to the extent that it does exist between art forms.) Of course, both "pure" and "impure" work is valid, but it is primarily the "impure" that you will find discussed here.

Even if nothing else derives from this book, I should like to disabuse those people who think that anyone who produces or finds great value in avant-garde work is abnormal, sick, or a charlatan. Sometimes, when a person cannot understand something, he is not able to believe that anyone else could be profoundly interested; avant-garde art is often seen as a trick or a "put-on." But I can assure you that this is not the case. I know personally almost every contemporary artist whom I discuss here. They are all deeply committed and honest people. None of them is trying to "kid" anyone. If my writing seems overly serious at times, remember those who do not take the avant-garde seriously enough.

MICHAEL KIRBY

New Paltz, New York
August 27, 1968

THE ART OF TIME

The
Art of Time:
The Aesthetics of
the Avant-Garde

There are those who say that the term "avant-garde" is obsolete, that it is no longer useful, that an art fitting the term no longer exists. This view is based on the proposition that an avant-garde artist is, by definition, one who is so far "ahead of his time" that his work is not accepted by society. Thus Cubism, the *Fauves*, Dada, and so forth were avant-garde at the time of their origins but are no longer, and, because the products of contemporary artists are generally accepted by the art world and at least a certain significant portion of the concerned public, there is no true avant-garde today.

If we follow strictly the definition I have sketched, there is certainly some truth in this conclusion. The public at large still rejects avant-garde work. Its tastes continue to cling to social realism in drama, representationalism in painting and sculpture, and the diatonic scale in music. But, except perhaps for theatre, there is a wide acceptance of avant-garde attitudes among those who are actively involved with the arts. I know only three or four artists who might in any way be considered to be important who are not able to show their work regularly at an established gallery. Whether this contemporary accept-ance of art is due to the socially "safe" quality of the work or to the greatly increased number of dealers, art publications, and educated members of the potential art public is not the ques-tion. It is true that the present social context of artistic creation is significantly more permissive and accepting than it was when the term "avant-garde" was first coined.* But since there does not seem to be a more fitting word to stand for the type of art with which I am concerned, I continue to use "avant-garde," although perhaps with some slight modification of meaning.

For one thing, "avant-garde" may still be used to describe those works of the late nineteenth and earlier twentieth cen-turies that did take some time to be accepted by society. Just as there is still usefulness in the names of the various move-ments of which it was composed, one may continue to refer to work as "avant-garde" even after it has become a basic ele-ment in most surveys of art history. In this sense, "avant-garde" becomes almost synonymous with "modern art," although "con-temporary art" would be a much larger category including artists of quite different and more traditional persuasions.

While the term "modern art" is flat and bland, however, "avant-garde" refers specifically to a concern with the historical *directionality* of art. An advance guard implies a rear guard or at least the main body of troops following behind. It is this attitude or belief in the directionality of art that is of primary

---

* In his brilliant book *The Banquet Years* subtitled *The Origins of the Avant-Garde in France 1885 to World War I* (New York: Doubleday & Co. Inc. 1961), p. 25, Roger Shattuck says, "Arbitrarily one can estab-lish the origin of the avant-garde in 1863, when Napoleon III consented to the Salon des Refusés."

importance. Some artists may accept the limits of art as defined, as known, as given; others may attempt to alter, expand, or escape from the stylistic aesthetic rules passed on to them by the culture. This impulse to redefine, to contradict, to continue the sensed directionality of art as far as they are able, is independent of success. The fact that an artist does not actually succeed in adding anything of importance to the historical development of art does not, in this sense, make the term "avant-garde" inapplicable. It is his intent or desire that is enough to separate him from those who do not share his goals and beliefs.

Nor is the acceptance or rejection of an artist's work by society sufficient grounds to determine correct use of the term. Directionality, or a belief in and concern with directionality, depends upon the creator and not upon the attitudes of society. Thus it is possible to say, without any contradiction in terms, that contemporary avant-garde art is generally accepted by society while that earlier work in which the beliefs were first manifested was not.

(On the negative side, there is a glamorous and romantic aura surrounding the French term that I do not intend to exploit in my usage. In many cases, this nostalgic romanticism seems to be the reason for the denial of its applicability to contemporary artists. What might be called "the Van Gogh syndrome" reasons that if an artist has not suffered, he cannot be of any worth; therefore, if society accepts the work without first punishing the creator with its rejection, the art is necessarily inferior. This is one way to "prove" the insignificance of work one does not like and to protect memories of the Good Old Days when artists, all of whom lived in garrets, were great, persecuted, heroic, and tormented.)

At any rate, it is quite obvious that standard aesthetic theory has little or no relevance to the art of the avant-garde. By "aesthetic theory" I do not mean art criticism, the discussion of styles of art, or the evaluation of particular works. This type of thought, much of it provided by the artists themselves, is quite abundant and, frequently, to the point. But present philosophical investigation and discussion of the broad principles of artistic appreciation are inadequate in the light of avant-garde work. It is this very inadequacy that gives rise to the use of such terms as "anti-art" and "non-art" when discussing the avant-garde. Since the work does not fit traditional explanations and codifications of the aesthetic experience, some new category is invented for it: Extant philosophical principles are protected by the too simple expedient of refusing to admit that the troublesome material falls into the same category as that which has already been used as the basis of long-held internally consistent theories.

The investigation by philosophy of the aesthetic experience must come after the fact, however. It cannot arbitrarily limit the area of investigation in order to arrive at results that it desires. Unless aesthetics explains the perception of all of art, it is of little intellectual or practical worth. Theory cannot contradict practice, and the total available data must fit the theories or the theories must be changed. For this reason, it is imperative to reexamine, reevaluate, and modify basic aesthetic theory in light of the avant-garde. This effort, when complete and detailed, should provide not only an aesthetic of the avant-garde but aesthetics that are based on, and applicable to, all art.

In discussing the inadequacy of "traditional aesthetics," I am not necessarily referring to the theories of any specific philosopher or philosophers but to what appear to be commonly held beliefs about the aesthetic experience. These general beliefs are given cogent shape by any number of theoretical writers, of course, but it is not my intent to criticize any one of them in detail. In most cases, such as that of empathy theory, it is not a question of abandoning the construct completely but of realizing that it has limited rather than universal application. Since existing theories were based upon particular works, they still retain limited validity in reference to those works, even though they cannot be given the fundamental pertinence that they claim.

To a certain extent, since it tends to determine and channel perceptions, such a new theory becomes polemic and didactic.

As I have said, however, the promulgation of particular value judgments is not the intent of this essay, and we are not directly concerned here with appreciation and evaluation. It should not be surprising that even the artists who are involved with the avant-garde do not agree among themselves about the artistic worth of particular pieces. (I can think of only two artists whose work as a whole has achieved an even approximately unanimous acceptance, for however brief a time, among my many friends and acquaintances who are artists.) From the sociopsychological point of view, anyone's reaction to a work of art is as "true" and "valid" as anyone else's, and it is too easy to see such critical discussion as the elevation of one person's experience at the expense of another's. We are concerned here with theories of art in general rather than with the details of appreciation of any one art.

But the avant-garde still stirs strong negative emotions, and many people (like John Simon, who states dramatically that "This may be the dark night of the arts") seem to reject modern art *in toto*. On this level contentiousness may be involved, and a new aesthetic adequately encompassing the products of the avant-garde should permit the values of that work to be seen more easily by those who were previously unable to do so. I certainly do not mean to claim, however, that anyone or everyone who accepts the avant-garde must, should, or does accept my formulations.

The term "avant-garde" does not, in itself, denote value. Avant-garde work per se is neither good nor bad. If we attempt to distance ourselves from the effect involved in the question, it would be logical to assume that the objective quality—if such a term has any meaning—or usual experience of avant-garde works would fall along a normal distribution curve with most of the pieces being "average" with quite small percentages registering as "near perfect" or "totally inadequate." The subjective reaction to this distribution might alter the labeling in more emotional directions, but this kind of distinction is not the purpose of the type of aesthetic theory with which we are concerned.

It is sufficient for our purposes to recognize that a significant

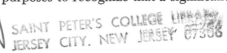

number of sufficiently normal people derive what they report to be intense aesthetic experiences from avant-garde work. This is a sociological fact. If these experiences cannot be explained by traditional aesthetic theory, modifications in that theory must be made to elucidate the general principles involved in the entire range of aesthetic experience.

1 | When discussing aesthetics, one is expected to begin with a definition of the word "art." The problem is clear: to provide a definition broad enough to include all that is considered art while clearly differentiating it from all that is not art. As has already been suggested, the question of definition would seem to be particularly important when considering avant-garde work, which is continually attempting to redefine the limits of art itself.

One useful definition is that which describes a work of art as *a man-made thing which has no objective practical or functional purpose*. It is obvious that only man creates art: It is not a natural occurrence, nor is it produced by animals.

Of course, this definition allows doodles, jewelry, fireworks, decoration, cartoons, and many other functionless creations to be called "art." Is there any reason to be concerned, however, if a definition does not categorically separate rock gardens and fountains from sculpture? If more subtle distinctions are needed, subcategories such as "commercial art," "popular art," "fine art," and so forth may be employed. After all, "art" is a word of neutral value. It does not mean that the particular work of art is either good or bad; a doodle may be merely considered "bad art" rather than being excluded from the category of "art."

But this is not the way we think when we say something is "not art." Being a work of art somehow seems important to us: Art is more worthwhile than non-art. Thus we deny the appellation "art" to anything that seems to us unimportant, trivial, or insignificant, whether it is a doodle or an avant-garde painting. This subjective personal reaction is, of course, what art is all about, but it cannot be used as a basis for definition, since there will never be any universal agreement on what is important or unimportant, significant or trivial. Personal taste is no grounds for determining what is, or is not, art.

This is really the problem that the concept of "fine art" attempts to solve: some art, that to which we are almost always referring when we use the word, is sensed to be of an entirely different order. Since we wish to consider only this type of creation, we may define a work of art as *a man-made thing of no objective practical or functional purpose that is intended to have aesthetic importance or significance.* In other words, since it is commonly accepted that art is important, man-made, and functionless, a thing is a work of art if it is intended as art.

This intent to achieve aesthetic importance or significance is entirely the concern of the creator, and the standards involved are his alone. Intention is not decided or determined by the observer. This limits the range of things with which we are concerned: Its creator does not claim significance for a doodle, but everything that is implicitly or explicitly proposed as significant art by an artist must be considered as art, whether or not we ourselves evaluate it as significant.

Thus, furniture, silverware, automobiles, rockets, and so forth are not art, even if we look at them as if they had no purpose. The observer does not convert something that has a practical purpose into a work of art merely by changing his attitude toward it. Duchamp did demonstrate with his "ready-mades," however, that a functional thing may become a work of art by being made functionless and placed in the context of art. It is not the physical characteristics or sensory impact of a man-made thing that determines whether or not it is art, but a factor that exists only in cognition: its purpose. This emphasis on the subjective aspects of experience rather than on the objective physical characteristics of the thing experienced will be a consistent concern of this essay.

As I pointed out a moment ago, status as art does not mean that the work is good art. A claim of importance does not mean that a thing is important. But it does differentiate the work from all those that make no such claim, limiting the field without recourse to personal judgment and giving us a starting point for a study of aesthetics. This study can be seen as little more than an explanation of the experiential context within which a work justifies or fails to justify its claim to importance and significance.

In one meaning of the word, "aesthetics" may be considered as the "philosophy of the beautiful," but the relationship of beauty and art now appears to be a thoroughly inconsistent one. Not all art is beautiful, nor is the presence of beauty enough to designate a creation as a work of art. To my mind, "beauty" has become a debased and almost meaningless word. One reason for this is that, although the experience of beauty is an entirely subjective thing, the implications of the word, strangely enough, have tended to become objective. Everyone knows that a sunset *is* beautiful. If I say to you, "She is a beautiful girl," it may not indicate any emotional reaction to the girl on my part but merely that I recognize the fact that her appearance falls within those clear limits of beauty that you and everyone else in our culture will recognize. This objectification may add to the reliability of communication, but it makes the word "beauty" trite and banal, hardly representative of the characteristics of the aesthetic experience that we wish to designate.

It could be said that flowers or a sunset are seen as beautiful because of their subtlety, variety, and intensity of color; an overcast sky at evening would not be beautiful because it lacked this kind of perceptual excitement. This view of beauty emphasizes the pleasure and appeal of pure sensory stimulation for its own sake. Although the appeal of art has traditionally been "for its own sake," it is precisely this view of aesthetic experience that I will argue against. Applied to art, this definition of beauty supports entertainment, excitement, titillation, and sensory pleasure as central values. Although useful as a contrast conception against which the basic nature of art may be seen, a purely sensory concept of beauty does not adequately explain the aesthetic experience.

In actuality, an overcast sky at evening might appear much

more beautiful than the most elaborate sunset to a farmer, for example, whose crops were in desperate need of rain. Even though we have defined art as being nonutilitarian, this practical sense of the word "beauty" does, I think, have some pertinence to the aesthetic experience, and I will return to it later. It suggests, for one thing, that the experience of a thing—in this case, the clouds—depends upon the total historical/personal context.

Since everyone knows that a sunset is beautiful, the implication, when applying the word to art, is that the aesthetic experience should be of the same sort. But exactly the opposite is true. The aesthetic experience is of an entirely different kind or order from the experience of nature. Although the perceptual mechanisms are identical, the results of the perception of art and non-art are not the same: It is these very differences that we want to study.

Thus the primary reason for rejecting the term "beauty" as of key importance in understanding the aesthetic experience is its common association with sensory pleasure. I am not sure that pleasure of any kind is a necessary aspect of the perception of art, even when the work is rated positively. In other words, it is conceivable that a piece can be seen as significant and meaningful without the viewer feeling pleasure.

Although I consider the nature of the aesthetic experience to be spiritual, I do not wish to argue the specific point here. Let us say that art seems to be a spiritual matter: It conveys the *feeling* that it functions at a basic level of existence. But spiritual experiences are not always pleasant ones, and St. John of the Cross, for example, suffered his "dark night of the soul." Art that is disturbing, disorienting, or repulsive can, theoretically, also be important and meaningful. At any rate, I think it best to consider pleasure, especially sensory pleasure, as merely a possible adjunct to the aesthetic experience. The creation of beauty and pleasure certainly do not define it.

One reason for the confusion of beauty in nature with what I will call, for the moment, "beauty in art" lies in the intensity of both experiences. Although introspective reporting remains a poor tool, it is all we have, and all subjective statements about art agree on an intensity of experience that distinguishes "good" art from "bad." But what is it that is felt intensely? Distinctions disappear and quantity tends to replace identity. Keats was apparently feeling this when he wrote his famous, "Beauty is truth, truth beauty." The subjective reaction to what is perceived as a truth can have great intensity, as can the reaction to the perception of beauty, although in neither case is the intensity a necessary or defining characteristic. When truth or beauty are perceived without this intensity of experience, they can be distinguished quite easily, but this is not true in their heightened states, when they are "all ye know on earth, and all ye need to know." This same kind of blurring of distinctions by heightened affect may explain the tendency to suppose that intense aesthetic experience is equivalent to the reaction to natural beauty.

Thus the key word in aesthetic theory is not "beauty," as has been suggested by traditional aesthetics, but "significance." The feeling or perception of significance may be mislabeled as "beauty," but the two are not the same. Let me emphasize that I am speaking now about significance as a *quality of perception* and not as a cognitive factor. Of course it may also exist as a cognitive element in the same way that beauty may be understood and known rather than felt, but it is significance as a quality of perception that can be seen as explaining the intensity of the aesthetic experience. As we indicated in our definition of art, the creation of art depends upon the artist's personal attempt to achieve what he feels to be significant. The experience of the finished product is also evaluated in terms of significance. It is with the aesthetic experience of the artist's product that we are primarily concerned. In order to understand it, we must first examine the sensory aspects of perception, even though we will find that the significance of art ultimately depends upon trans-sensory aspects of experience.

2 | There is a universally held but inaccurate concept or model of the aesthetic experience. This model posits a single correct

way of perceiving an art object; the simultaneous and intrinsic value attributes of that correct perception are, of course, also correct. This model is usually, but not necessarily, identical with a person's own experience. In other words, the concept postulates a single, objective truth about a work of art, and if we, as individuals, do not perceive it completely (as we usually feel we do) then it is still available to us. If we do have wrong perceptions, they may be corrected.

As we grow older we find that our experiences of, and opinions about, specific works of art change. According to the model, we have had incorrect experiences and are now having correct ones. But the feeling of correctness—as opposed, for example, to a student's possible acceptance of incorrectness because of his willingness to learn—does not guarantee correctness. Frequently, an experience that we feel certain is right is replaced somewhat later by another significantly different but equally correct experience of the same work of art. Looking back at our past aesthetic experiences, we often feel that they were incorrect and that we now perceive the truth, although the degree of certainty is no greater now than it was previously. At every moment the true, objective aesthetic work seems revealed to us, but these truths are not consistent through time nor, as nearly as we can determine, do they usually agree with others' perceptions of the same work. Even at the present moment, a single sense may contradict itself. Locke and Berkeley both referred to the experiment in which one hand is placed in hot water and the other hand in cold water for several minutes, and then both hands are put into water of moderate temperature: The same water feels cold to one hand and warm to the other—a clear demonstration of the relativity of perception and value.

The *feeling* of correctness in aesthetic judgment is self-contradictory and impossible to verify. Actually, the concept or model is false; the single correct way of perceiving a work of art, and the single correct set of value attributes coexistent in that experience, do not exist.

Just as a person who does not believe in free will still experiences life—unless he is psychotic—as if he had free will, an intellectual *belief* in the subjectivity of value does not prevent a person from *feeling* the truth of the incorrect model I have sketched. Although everyone feels that value is objective, a person may simultaneously believe in its subjectivity. This is not intended as merely a philosophical statement. Since an artist's beliefs obviously determine the character of the work he produces, I am attempting to discuss those questions which seem to have specific practical relevance to the expansion of art by the avant-garde. In other words, a belief among artists in the subjectivity of values would be functional *whether or not* it was philosophically correct. The rest of my discussion of aesthetics is presented in this same spirit: While attempting to establish an intellectual position that I believe is true, I am also endeavoring to document—by analogy, if you prefer to evade the philosophical issues—certain generative factors in modern art.

The objectification of perception—the feeling that the world is as it appears to be—has been called "phenomenal absolutism." In *The Influence of Culture on Visual Perception*, Marshall H. Segall, Donald T. Campbell, and Melville J. Herskovits write:

The normal observer naïvely assumes that the world is exactly as he sees it. He accepts the evidence of perception uncritically. He does not recognize that his visual perception is *mediated* by indirect inference systems. . . .

Socially, one important aspect of phenomenal absolutism is the observer's assumption that all other observers perceive the situation as he does, and that if they respond differently it is because of some perverse willfulness rather than because they act on different perceptual content.*

Although I shall concentrate on the trans-sensory aspects of aesthetic experience, sensory perception should be mentioned

---

* From *The Influence of Culture on Visual Perception* by Marshall H. Segall, Donald T. Campbell, and Melville J. Herskovits, copyright © 1966 by the Bobbs-Merrill Company, Inc. Reprinted by permission of the publishers.

first. The authors of *The Influence of Culture on Visual Perception*—an important presentation of basic concepts with an extensive bibliography on the psychological and cultural aspects of perception—believe that their studies demonstrate that human perception is culturally influenced. They found that people in different cultures were differentially susceptible to certain geometric illusions. This means that culture can change not merely the meaning and interpretation of what is seen but the actual perception itself. Although their work is not conclusive, and more investigation must be done, it is a provocative attempt to investigate an area where "pure" data are very difficult to obtain.

If any of the senses is studied through psychophysical measurement, individual differences in perception become apparent. If any continuum of objective physical stimuli is correlated with the perception-reactions to those stimuli, the variety of response is one of its most apparent aspects. Take, for example, the relationship between the change in the physical intensity of light entering the eye and the observed change in brightness. Obviously, some measurable change in brightness will not be perceived by any human being. Although quite marvelous, the human eye, even discounting "noise" in the nerve system, is not perfect. The amount of increase or decrease in intensity that is needed before a change is perceived will actually vary from person to person. How, then, can judgments of "correct" and "incorrect" response be made? All of us are "wrong" at one physical level, because we see no change in brightness when a change in intensity is actually occurring; a few people, whose eyes are the most sensitive to brightness of any in the human race, are "correct" when they perceive changes that no one else can, and everyone else is "incorrect"; and so forth. It is possible, of course, to calculate averages and set up norms, but this is not quite the same thing.

Or consider so-called color blindness. Some people think that it exists only in such dramatic forms as the inability to distinguish red from green. Red/green color blindness is the most common form and occurs in over five per cent of men and less than one per cent of women, but there is also an entirely different type of deficiency in the perception of color that affects men and women equally. Most simply, this *anomalous color vision* is a reduction in sensitivity to one or more of the three basic color systems (red, green, and blue) that are involved in perception. One result, apparently, is that people with color anomaly cannot distinguish as many or as subtle saturation changes within a particular hue, for example, as can people with normal color vision. It is important to note that it has been estimated that as much as twenty per cent of the population— one out of every five—is "color weak" in one way or another.

Since these weaknesses show up as variations in threshold-level discriminations, they are very difficult to determine without precision equipment. While the inability to distinguish red from green becomes apparent when merely trying to obey a traffic signal light, the question of whether an unsaturated blue-gray can be distinguished from a slightly more saturated blue-gray, for example, is not as available to everyday experience. Many people are color deficient without knowing it; it would be entirely possible to go through life without becoming aware that you had anomalous color vision.

In my senior year at college, I was doing an experimental thesis on "The depth effects of color," and I wanted to pretest each of the subjects in order to exclude any who did not have normal color vision. I found that in administering the test plates, in which numbers can be read in a field of colored dots if you have normal vision, I had to use the key to see if the answers were correct. Although I had absolutely no hint of it previously, I found at the age of 22 that I was color deficient. Except for the necessity of taking the test, I might never have known of this anomalous color vision.

In spite of these facts, it is somewhat startling to learn that even the most striking forms of color blindness were not discovered until the nineteenth century by a chemist, John Dalton, who found that he was unable to distinguish between certain chemicals that could be visually differentiated only on the basis of color. The point is that a color blind (or color deficient) person is not really blind; he sees something. We learn that the sky is blue, the clouds are white, the trees and grass are green, and so forth. But there are cues other than color for recognizing the sky, clouds, and trees, and if you can make color discriminations that I cannot, we still agree on terminology. I call the sky "blue" and the clouds "white," and any difference in the quality of perception will not be indicated by difficulties in, or a breakdown of, communication. The industrial revolution and the rise of science brought with them widespread specific informational use of color and increased the possibility that deviations from the norm in color perception would be discovered, but still the subtleties of anomalous color vision are seldom manifest in everyday life.

The point is that even on the most basic level of aesthetic experience, that of the purely sensory, we may expect a great variety in perceptual response to the same work of art. The fact that almost all of this variation occurs within a relatively narrow and subtle range does not matter. Theoretically, no difference can be dismissed as insignificant, and a difference in perception must always be related to, or cause, a difference in aesthetic response. In addition, the total variation in any situation increases geometrically as more than one dimension of the experience is taken into account—as the parameters of brightness, color perception, visual acuity, astigmatism, and so forth are all considered as part of the purely sensory perception of a painting, for example. Whether or not we all see the same painting depends upon the standards that are used. Compared to Ted Williams, the famous baseball player—about whom one of his hunting companions is reported to have said, "He can tell what kind of ducks they are before we can see any ducks."—most of us demonstrate sensory deficiency.

If sensory receptors are physically unable to register and transmit particular objective stimuli, the universality of the experience breaks down at a very basic level. Another level at which the same thing can happen is that where the sensory information is "translated" from the neural code into experience. Two exactly identical neural messages may be experienced differently. With the addition of subjective meaning to the sensory input, the same encoding may have many possible manifestations as experience.

When a small dot of light is viewed from a distance in a completely dark room, it will appear to move even though it is actually stationary. The rate, direction, distance, and pattern of the perceived movement varies from person to person. This is known as the autokinetic effect, a phenomenon that has yet to be fully explained although many have tried. Experiments have shown that the reported perceptions of the autokinetic effect change when the judgments are made in a group rather than alone. The individuals in the group tend to see the movements in the same way as they are reported by others. Since there is nothing with which to compare the size of the light, its distance and movement, estimates or standards are more readily adopted or learned from others. Each group develops its own more or less common opinion about the movement of the light.

Interior and exterior validation are both irrelevant in this case. Since the movement of the light, which is ostensibly controlled by the experimenter, could actually be changing from observation to observation, a subject is not aware that his perception when viewing alone has later changed to conform with that of the other subjects. And since the light actually remains stationary, one judgment of movement cannot be considered more correct than another.

In the same way, the famous distorted rooms used in experiments by Adalbert Ames, Jr., show that the same objective stimulus can be seen in different ways by the same person and that perception is related to learning. When a person looks into the viewing window of one of the Ames's rooms, he sees, for example, an apparently normal room with doors indicated on the side walls and two windows represented on the rear wall. But strange things happen in the room. A boy standing at the right seems much taller than a man standing at the left, although both are normally proportioned. The apparent size of inanimate things placed in the room is also distorted, and a chair, in this case, placed at the left looks much smaller than one placed at the right.

Actually it is the room that is distorted: In the example I have described, the rear wall, which appears to be perpendicular to the observer's line of sight, actually slopes away from right to left. The room is built in false perspective, so that the image on the viewer's retina is the same as that which would be created by a rectangular room. Our habit of interpreting this particular retinal configuration as being "a rectangular room" is so strong that it persists in spite of the size contradictions that occur. Because of the apparent shape of the room and their relationship to it, two people or things of equal size are seen at the same apparent distance even though one is actually much closer than the other; rather than appearing closer, the nearer figure seems much larger than the more distant one. The illusion of linear perspective creating a diminution in size as the distance from the observer increases has become "real."

Ames's distorted room experiments demonstrate, among other things, the point at which experience ceases to be merely sensory and takes on trans-sensory aspects. The gestalt or retinal configuration or pattern—in this case the false perspective lines of the room—may still be thought of as sensory material, but the meaning of the particular gestalt is shown to be dependent upon additional factors. It is these additional, trans-sensory elements that become of major significance in the perception of art. There seems to be no doubt that learning has much to do with them. Just as it was established by learning, the meaning or interpretation of the retinal configuration may be changed through learning. By touching the distorted room and its contents with a long pole or by bouncing a ball back and forth in it, the observer may teach himself to see the actual shape and the true relationships involved.

If there are grounds for questioning whether, on a purely sensory level, any two of us perceive the physical world in exactly identical ways, the assumption that there is one correct set of value attributes related to any particular work of art is more obviously unjustified. This is not the place to discuss in detail the character and development of values, but one interesting experiment, which Elliot Aronson and J. Merrill Carlsmith conducted with four- and five-year-old children, illustrates something of the manner in which values are created, formed, or introjected.

The experimenters asked their young subjects to rate a number of toys on their attractiveness. Then they selected one of the toys designated as very attractive by each child and told him he could not play with it. Half of the children were threatened with mild punishment if they played with the toy, and half were told they would be punished severely. The experimenters left the room; none of the children played with the forbidden toys. When the children were again asked to rate the attractiveness of all the toys, a striking and significant thing happened: Those children who had been promised severe punishment still rated the forbidden toys as high as, or even higher than, the preliminary rating, while those who had been threatened with mild punishment found the forbidden toy much less attractive than they had previously.

There are many implications of this experiment, but the point I want to emphasize is that the new values that were created in half of the children—the low attractiveness of the chosen toys—were no less true or real than the previous high rating of the same toy. In each case the rating was an indication of how the child really felt about the toy. The fact that we can find a direct cause, in the experimenters' behavior, for the change in values does not invalidate the experience or cause the quality to change. The same is true of the values felt in art. One cause is no more valid or correct than another. All values are real.

(To oversimplify, the learning of new values took place in this case primarily with those children who, because of the mildness of the threat, could not successfully explain to themselves why they did not want to play with the forbidden toys. Those who were threatened with severe punishment were quite clear in their minds why they refrained from playing with the toys, and they retained their previous values or frustration made the toys seem even more desirable. This is merely one of the more subtle aspects of value formation, and even though it is not difficult mentally to substitute "works of art" for "toys" and contemplate the functioning of the mechanism in relation to art, the purpose of mentioning the experiment is not to explain specifically any particular example of aesthetic experience but to establish the basic fact that values are learned.)

In final contrast to traditional aesthetics that posits an identical sensory experience for every observer or listener is the wide variety of perceptual variations that actually result from the time factor involved in the appreciation of every art. A painting is not seen completely in one glance. The eye moves from point to point, from detail to larger view; it hesitates, changes speed, skips sections, and doubles back to make comparisons. There is no strict control or rule determining the length or characteristics of this process. Composition of various sorts is supposed to "guide the eye," but this, at best, only creates certain likely possibilities; it may be thought of as governing the *average* reaction to some extent, but it cannot eliminate the wide variation in individual responses.

The implication of traditional aesthetics is that a painting has an objective reality that can be studied until it is completely apprehended. Thus any two people who look at a painting until it is "all perceived" have identical and correct responses. But this is like saying that two columns of numbers are the same because their sum is the same; the aesthetic experience does not work by addition. Once the eye has followed a certain visual path over a painting at a certain rate, for example, this movement becomes a unique part of the total aesthetic experience, qualifying everything that comes after it. These variations in the total experience are subtle. Perhaps for practical purposes they may be ignored. But from a theoretical point of view, they are very important and must be recognized as another factor that causes a great variety in the aesthetic experience.

These perceptual differences are not eliminated from such forms as drama and music that use time in a more conscious and controlled manner. Each member of an audience perceives the work from a different distance and angle; each is free at any moment to focus his attention on particular details at the expense of the whole. Even in film, which comes as close as possible to presenting the same sensory data at each performance, the viewer may examine each image with the same kind of variation in visual focus and emphasis that exists in the perception of a painting.

Thus in this section I have touched on some of the perceptual, cognitive, and valuative aspects of the aesthetic experience in terms of their distribution and variation and in terms of their relationship to learning. By indicating the variation and equivalency of perceptions at every level of experience, I am emphasizing a relativistic concept of art in contrast to the traditional independent or objective one. By discussing learning, I am stressing the particular relationship of the total perception to things, events, and states that preceded it rather than to the sensory data of which it is also composed; the aesthetic experience is placed in the continuum of time rather than entirely in the perceptual present.

One category of objects we call "works of art," and, as R. L. Gregory wrote in *Eye and Brain:*

The seeing of objects involves many sources of information beyond those meeting the eye when we look at an object. It generally involves knowledge of the object derived from previous experience, and this experience is not limited to vision but may include the other senses; touch, smell, hearing, and perhaps also temperature or pain. Objects are far more than patterns of stimulation: objects have pasts and futures; when we know its past or can guess its future, an object transcends experience and becomes an embodiment of knowledge and expectation . . .*

In the next section, we will examine ways in which works of art "transcend" direct sensory experience to become embodiments of knowledge and expectation.

---

* From *Eye and Brain: The Psychology of Seeing* by R. L. Gregory, copyright © 1966 by the author and used with the permission of McGraw-Hill Book Company.

3 | Another completely unsatisfactory concept put forward by traditional aesthetics is that the experience of art is hermetic, sealed off, as it were, from any connection with the rest of life. According to this view, art is perceived "for itself alone." Its appreciation employs a detachment and psychical distance unlike that involved in everyday existence. The following quotations, taken almost at random, illustrate the wide acceptance of this point: "But only the sensuous appearance of the aesthetic object . . . is attended to in aesthetic contemplation" (Theodor Lipps); We experience on object aesthetically "when we look at it . . . without relating it, intellectually or emotionally, to anything outside of itself" (Erwin Panofsky); "Every real work of art has a tendency to appear thus dissociated from its mundane environment" (Suzanne Langer); ". . . to appreciate a work of art we need bring with us nothing from life, no knowledge of its ideas and affairs, no familiarity with its emotions . . ." (Clive Bell).

I do not mean to deny that a hermetic and "pure" aesthetic experience is possible. That is, it seems to be possible. Most of us have had it many times. But if we carefully limit our attention and clear our minds in order to attend only to the sensuous appearance of the aesthetic object and do not relate it, intellectually or emotionally, to anything outside of itself, this is only an alteration in consciousness. The human mechanism is still functioning, and most of this functioning occurs on an unconscious level. In the unconscious, the person is far from hermetic. When we describe the broad context of the aesthetic experience in this section, it should be remembered that most of the aesthetic experience is produced at this unconscious level. In other words, being in a pure hermetic state of aesthetic contemplation does not mean that the unconscious is functioning hermetically. This would be impossible. Therefore the hermetic state has little meaning when considering the whole perceptual system, and does not, in fact, exist at the most crucial levels.

Anything may be looked at "aesthetically." The hermetic aesthetic consciousness can be adopted in order to experience any object or action. The chosen thing is then seen "for itself alone" with no reference to function or practicality. This demonstrates that the traditional hermetic experience derives as much from the perceiver as from the nature of the work of art. It is self-induced. It is emotionally "inflated" by personal manipulation of areas of attention and a habituated control of affect. It is determined by social traditions and learned by the individual, relying to a good extent on devices that are quite comparable to self-hypnosis, semi-trance states, autosuggestion, and various contemplative devices that limit consciousness. After all, the Eastern contemplative adept is apparently successful in erasing all but the fact of consciousness itself.

It is my position that the hermetic consciousness is not a necessary condition for experiencing art. Since it has been dominant in our culture for some time, many works have been, and are being, produced to be experienced in this way. There is no reason why these works should not be contemplated, at least part of the time, in that state for which they were conceived. But not all art is meant to be experienced in this way.

The fact that a pure state of so-called aesthetic appreciation can exist does not mean that it should be adopted for the experiencing of all art, nor does its existence, in itself, validate or justify the theories to which it is linked. The separation of the traditional aesthetic experience from everyday life makes it seem precious, escapist, and romantic. Its autocontrolled aspects make it seem arbitrary and overly self-indulgent.

Art, in a perceptual sense, is no different from non-art things and objects. It does not require a different perceptual state. It does not need to be looked at with a mental attitude or set unlike that involved in everyday life. It is not hermetic.

(I must emphasize that this does not mean that there is no difference between art and life. The mere fact that a thing is art makes it quite different from the other things we experience. But this is a mental distinction, not a perceptual one; it does not depend on a particular way of looking at the world. Exactly how the knowledge that a thing is art brings transsensory elements into existence that are not present in the experiencing of other objects will be discussed later in this section.)

In general, we may equate the hermetic aesthetic experience of "the thing for its own sake" with perception at a sensory level as was discussed in the last section. In this section, we will consider what can be called the "trans-sensory" aspects of the aesthetic experience. The "purity" of the traditional aesthetic experience is achieved by the repression or the rejection from consciousness of these elements. Only later, in reflection and cogitation, are they permitted into awareness as aspects of a different and nonaesthetic state. But it is important to understand that these factors come into play automatically on an unconscious level. The trans-sensory aspects of perception therefore function even in the traditional hermetic state. They operate whether we are aware of them or not. The elaboration and exploitation of these elements by consciousness gives the "open" or non-hermetic state an entirely different character, however. Thus the discussion of the trans-sensory elements of experience applies just as well to the traditionally defined aesthetic experience as it does to the more open one that I propose.

Especially since we learn how to see and hear, life is always the ground against which a work of art is experienced. Art is always perceived in terms of life. The hermetic attitude does not contradict this but merely prevents consciousness from "flowing back" into life, so to speak. The person feels "cut off" from real life, even though this is not actually the case. In reality, life exists as a contrast conception to art. The formal differences between art and life can be important aspects of experience, and they would not be known if the experience were truly hermetic. Conscious attention to this comparison and contrast of a work of art with all aspects of life naturally produces experience of a different quality from when the process is entirely unconscious. There is no reason, however, why only the latter should be considered "aesthetic."

Observable qualities—that is to say, the sensory aspect of a piece—may be modified in experience by trans-sensory informational elements. I have stated, as an aesthetic axiom not requiring proof, the fact that two sensory perceptions that differ in any respect will have different value attributes in an individual's experience. But the rule "Two objects that do not differ in any observable qualities cannot differ in aesthetic value," stated by Monroe C. Beardsley in his book *Aesthetics,* is not axiomatic. Information may change the character of an experience, making it quite different from another even though the sensory material is identical. The identity of the creator, for example, is often not an intrinsic sensory part of the work, and yet the knowledge can greatly influence the perception of the work; a rose by any other name might not smell as sweet.

As long ago as 1935, M. Sherif demonstrated experimentally that subjects tended to rank short prose passages, all actually written by the same person although ascribed to different authors, in accordance with their own previously given rating of the authors. In other words, a subject's previous appreciation of an author's work or his opinion of the author's position significantly affected his evaluation of the work.

(At the same time, Sherif also demonstrated that the prestige effect could be overcome statistically by "special effort." This effort is the same as that used in creating the hermetic aesthetic state. The psychic action in this state not only imposes another level of functioning on the perceptual one, but a misinterpretation of the effort may, when added to the basic unreality of the situation, be partly responsible for the heightened affect. At any rate, "correction" of experience is conscious and would not operate on unconscious elements.)

The influence of this same factor on perception is demonstrated by forgeries. For seven years "Christ and the Disciples at Emmaus" by Johannes Vermeer of Delft hung in the Boymans Museum in Rotterdam, admired as a great work of art by thousands of visitors. Abraham Bredius, one of the leading experts on Vermeer, called it "*the* masterpiece" of the artist. Then, in 1945, Han van Meegeren admitted having forged it and other "masterpieces." The whole experience of these works changed. They no longer generated the intense aesthetic response that they had previously, although their observable qualities were unchanged. At least I prefer to consider the change in experience an aesthetic one. Traditional aesthetics would claim that *aesthetically* the experience remained the same, and the "nonaesthetic" aspects of experience were what was altered. This distinction is crucial, and I will return to the point later. For now I will only suggest that the "extirpation" or rejection of the artist's identity from the total experience is unnecessary, artificial, and extremely difficult.

Knowing an artist's name means, in part, that while we are perceiving his work, we are remembering, to some extent, whether conscious of it or not, all of his other works to which we have been exposed. We recognize a particular artist's style. We see the present work in terms of his past works. It is common to feel that such cumulative data make any particular artistic creation easier to understand and interpret: An artist's goal or purpose, for example, seems much easier to perceive by comparing works covering a span of time and implying directionality than it does from a single work. Additions from whatever level of memory and neural trace certainly make the experience "larger" and more complex. With the consideration of recognition and memory, we have entered into the crucial historical context of art. I am not referring now to the learning processes that were mentioned earlier. Learning, of course, is also historical but functions primarily as a structuring device, determining our perceptions and their meanings, among other things. The historical elements to which I want to draw attention now function as contrast conceptions: They are the bases for comparisons of various kinds made between the past and the present. Obviously, *a work of art may have meaning and significance not in terms of its sensory body alone but in comparisons to some other work or works.* (The two works that are thus compared could both be presented directly to experience—it is a simple matter to compare paintings hung next to each other in a museum, for example—but memory almost always provides one element, and the phenomenon may be considered as primarily a historical one.)

Let us say that a painter makes a reference to a work by another artist. He basically adopts the other painter's subject matter or style and makes changes or modifications. These changes or modifications become part of the aesthetic material of the work, but they can only be perceived if the other work is also seen or remembered: Two sets of data are needed to indicate a difference. Thus a "third quality" can be created by the comparison of two works of art. This comparison quality does not lie directly in the sensuous appearance of a single work itself, but it is the result of the comparison of that work with a second. These comparison qualities may exist in any dimension of the work: the subject matter, the forms and shapes in space and time, the ways of perceiving the world, and so forth.

Although the intended comparison of a work of art with only one other work is possible and gives the clearest model for the concept, the situation is hardly ever that explicit or limited. Most frequently, the contrast element against which a work is perceived is a particular style or even the total field of the art form itself.

Thus we have the concept of "the new" that is so fundamental to the avant-garde. Newness is a contrast conception. It exists only in the difference between things, and it is not visible in consciousness if, as directed by traditional aesthetics, a work is seen "for itself alone." This is not to suggest a value judgment: The new is not good merely because it is new, and the question of significance will be taken up in a later section. The new, however, can be an element in the total aesthetic experience. It and other trans-sensory comparison factors are intentionally employed by many artists and recognized by many people in their appreciation of the work. Allowances must be made for them in any realistic and accurate aesthetic theory.

Obviously, whether or not a particular element is perceived as new depends upon the individual. What is new to one person is not new to another. The same thing is true for other contrast elements. They depend for their perception upon the unique psychological field or ground against which they are seen. Thus they are different from person to person. Even two experiences of the same unchanging work by the same person may be quite different because the psychological context that creates these elements has changed. But the fact that contrast elements are not objectively fixed does not alter their importance. They are still elements of the aesthetic experience. As such they have the possibility of engendering positive or negative values, depending upon the taste of the perceiver.

It should not be inferred that contrast elements are created by the artist only as a result of conscious intent. The factors governing creativity are unconscious to a great extent, and there is no reason why an artist would have to believe in the principle of comparison factors before they could be found in his work. The same holds true for appreciation. Contemporary criticism stresses comparisons very heavily. It discusses, for example, the "dialectics" of modern painting and sculpture as works "comment on" each other. But the perception of contrast elements does not need to reach consciousness in order to register as part of the experience. There is no reason why newness or any of the other contrast factors could not be noted and evaluated without any conscious awareness of the factor.

In some respects, a contrast effect is like an afterimage. What is seen later depends upon what was looked at earlier: The contrast element in the total perception of the work of art or a moving red dot, for example, depends upon the work that formed the first half of the comparison or the green dot that caused the afterimage. In these terms, the process can be seen as historically unidirectional, moving from the past to the present. Newness depends upon the "subtraction" of all earlier work from the particular current work being perceived and this process is not reversible. The later is not "subtracted" from the earlier. Thus if the quality of newness or innovation exists, it continues to exist relative to its own place in history and cannot be taken away by later works. (Although the perceived significance of the innovation may, of course, change.) Newness may be measured at any point in the historical continuum and not just at the present moment, but such measurements are always made in the direction of later compared to earlier.

Actually, there is a contrast element that is measured in the opposite direction—against the current of time, so to speak. Similarities of later work to earlier work are perceived as what could be called "influence." (I use the word to indicate a comparison quality and do not mean to imply that only perceptual similarities are necessary to establish actual influence. Other historical facts such as availability would be necessary in addition to priority in time sequence.) The influence of a work on other works is, interestingly enough, a quality that does not exist in a newly completed work, but which may accumulate as the work ages.

From this point of view it is nonsense to look at, say, Picasso's "Les Demoiselles d'Avignon," painted in 1907, as if it had just been completed. Viewed hermetically, "outside of time," it only seems tentative, incomplete, and drably colored. In the context of time, the influence that this single painting has had on perception can create an intense feeling. All of its "pure" characteristics take on entirely different values in terms of historical aesthetics. This does not mean that the comparison qualities of influence need to be considered consciously. Cerebration is not necessary in order to perceive the influence of the past on the present.

Thus the date of a work's creation is another of the informational elements that, like knowledge of the author's identity, place the perception in its complete context. Whether the dating derives from figures carved into a piece of sculpture, from a printed card hanging next to the work in a museum, from published material, or from the resources of memory, it becomes an important catalyst and an intrinsic part of the aesthetic experience.

Among the other information about the work of art that can become part of the aesthetic experience is the history and data of a work's creation. I remember, for example, the girl who dismissed one of Jasper Johns's major works as "just old paint brushes stuck into a can." She had not looked carefully enough to see that the piece had actually been cast from a can filled with brushes and then painted to resemble the original. Even so, the fact that the particular material was bronze, important to the aesthetic appreciation of the piece, was unavailable to her visually—although in this case it could be found in the title: "Painted Bronze."

In order to make his "Stoppages-Etalon," Marcel Duchamp dropped three threads, each one meter in length, from a height of one meter and fastened them in position. The knowledge of his procedure is crucial to an appreciation of the work, but it cannot be obtained from the sensory study of the piece itself. In a like manner, information about methods, techniques, materials, and creative history of any work may be important, although they are not necessarily so.

Thus we can distinguish between traditional aesthetics and what could be called the "historical" or "situational" aesthetics suggested by the work of the avant-garde. Traditional aesthetics asks a particular hermetic attitude or state of mind that concentrates on the sensory perception of the work "for its own sake" and is different from that used in daily life. Historical aesthetics makes use of no special attitude or set, and art is viewed just as anything else in life. In this way, everything pertinent in any way to the work of art and the perception of it becomes part of the "aesthetic experience." The experience can therefore be seen as open rather than hermetic and as including factors that are considered "nonaesthetic" by traditional theory. The aesthetic experience can then be defined as any experience in which the attention is focused on a work of art.

But the simple awareness that the object of perception is a work of art gives the experience a particular character that is different from the experience of non-art objects. This is not a sensory distinction. If one imaginatively substitutes a non-art object or action for art, the experience will not be the same, if only because of the artificiality and pretense involved. Art is life, but life cannot be art. An object seen as a work of art is psychologically placed in a cultural-historical context that determines the characteristics of the experience. Traditional aesthetics asks that the perception of a work of art exist "outside of time," as it were. Situational or historical aesthetics sees the work in the context of time where the trans-sensory elements are of fundamental importance.

4 | The concept of "art as communication" is another aspect of traditional aesthetics that has to be abandoned in the light of modern psychology and avant-garde art. This concept posited the artist as "sender" and the person experiencing the work as "receiver" of a "message" about life. The artist was "trying to say something." If difficulties occurred in transmission of the message, they were due to either the artist's inadequacies in expression or the receiver's imperfect reception or understanding. This is a very simplified model, but even the most sophisticated communication theory does not apply to all art. It may apply to some art, of course, and some artists certainly attempt to communicate, but it is now realized that the model we have described is an inaccurate one and that the attempt to communicate is unnecessary.

At least since psychoanalysis, it has been apparent that not all of the "message" in a work of art is intentional. We now know that there is also a "latent content," to use the term that Freud applied to the analysis of dreams, and that the unconscious, as well as consciousness, gives form to the work of art. The work may still be seen as a message sent from the complete psyche of the artist, but this is communication in which the sender himself does not know the message. Any creation of man is seen as expressive, whether or not it is a work of art. The model begins to break down.

If the concept of communication is retained with its nonrational adjuncts, the psychoanalyst becomes the best possible and most efficient receiver, interpreting the unconscious elements of the work and "understanding" the complete message. But even psychoanalysts seem to read different messages in the same work. Their own discipline has pointed out subjective mechanisms such as projection that tend to register the message that the unconscious wants to register; just as "noise" is added to visual data by the optic nerve, the message is determined in part by the psychological characteristics of the human receiver.

The third place that our model of communication breaks down is in the message itself. A message is a symbolic construct: That which is present refers to that which is absent. All representational art is symbolic, in this sense, and can certainly be considered as communication. But abstract art may not be symbolic at all; it may merely be itself. A work of art may intend no external reference.

This, of course, does not eliminate the possibility of a "message" being received. Anything may be seen as a symbol. Any line, color, shape, or even a blank canvas, can be interpreted as having philosophical reference at some level. The Rorschach inkblots used in projective testing of personality have no intentional references; they are merely inkblots, but many different "messages" are "received" from them. Thus the "message" quality of an experience can be seen to depend in part upon the set or readiness of the receiver to perceive a message. If you look for a message in anything, you will see one. If art is believed to be communication, it will appear to be communication, even though the artist is not intending to create a symbol or send a message.

I do not mean to imply that symbolic interpretation of a work is necessarily wrong, even when it is understood that no reference of any sort was intended. We certainly cannot limit ourselves to the artist's intent. Any work, in a sense, becomes in part an open-ended metaphor: The work is *like* anything on any level of consciousness with which we want to compare it. A certain abstract painting, for example, may be compared to a particular event in history, to the emotions at a certain time of day, to social relationships, to the structure of the universe, or to life itself—to anything that the mind can conceive. If the comparison seems to be meaningful and important, it cannot be considered wrong or improper. At the same time, interpretation and the analogy of a work to something other than itself should not be considered as a necessity; the work may exist only on a perceptual level.

5 | Art *seems* to be significant. One of the most salient characteristics of the aesthetic experience is the impression or feeling of significance. In the first section I distinguished between art and other nonfunctional man-made creations such as decorations and entertainments on the basis of an intention in art to achieve significance. But to feel the significance of something is not the same thing as being able to demonstrate that significance objectively. The intent to embody significance does not mean that it is achieved.

Significance cannot be argued on the basis of one person's experience. What is significant to one person is not significant to another, and the reasons that an individual feels that significance exists in a work are a psychological question. Experience is very complex, and there could be as many different reasons that significance was sensed in a particular work as there were people who indicated they perceived the quality. If a work of art does have objective significance, it is obvious that that significance does not necessarily correlate directly with individual experience.

The traditional attitude is that since values seem to be objective, they are objective. This objectivity of value has never been satisfactorily demonstrated. At the same time, traditional aesthetics states that the values of a work are unrelated to practical life and lie only in the experience itself. This is consistent with the hermetic view that art is separate from life: Its significances are of its own order and are not related to mundane existence. (Since one historical view of the spirit separates it rather rigorously from the things of this world, my own earlier identification of art with spiritual concerns might seem to follow this line of thought, but I was merely using the word as indicative of the apparent depth and personal quality of the aesthetic experience—as a synonym, in other words, for the most intense and private kind of perceived significance.) Although it cannot yet be proved, however, I believe that art does have a kind of objective significance based in culture.

Before going into the question of objective significance, certain false standards must be pointed out. Some people see anything that is well-done as "art." Thus they have the art of juggling, the art of blowing glass, the art of playing chess, and so forth. Our definition of art in the opening section excluded most of these possibilities. But there are those who would attribute significance to works of art, as included in our definition, on the basis of whether or not they are well-made or well-done. Craft, technique, and talent are sometimes mistaken for significance.

I still remember the young girl at the old Whitney Museum on Eighth Street who, on seeing a large painting by Franz Kline, called gleefully to the elderly woman who was accompanying her, "Oh, I could do that!" If she had really known the technical requirements of the work, I doubt whether she would have acted superior. But the little girl implied that Kline's painting was not significant because it was, or seemed, easy to do. The attitude is common.

Today many artists have their work manufactured commercially by artisans and fabricators, and the little girl could certainly emulate one of their works merely by telling the craftsman what she wanted or by making a simple sketch. Technically, any carpenter could do some modern sculpture. But there is no reason that an artist actually has to make the physical work himself as long as he determines its characteristics. The point is that the ease with which a work of art is made (or the apparent ease with which it is made) has nothing to do with the significance of the work.

Nor does technique make a work important. Admiration may certainly be involved. We tend to envy things we cannot do ourselves and to "do" them through empathy, getting a kind of excitement out of vicariously accomplishing the extremely difficult. But admirable qualities are not the same as significance.

To relate talent to significance rests upon the same kind of assumptions. Talent means the natural ability, as opposed to learned or acquired ability, to do a particular thing well. This does not mean that a person without very much talent cannot accomplish as much as a person with a great amount of talent. Many other factors are involved. And the definition of the par-

ticular talent obviously depends upon the specific characteristics of the thing that is done. Once a human activity is clearly
delimited, the talent related to it may be perceived. We can
speak of a talent for running, or dancing, or drawing, and so
forth. But when it becomes a question of innovation, the known
and previously established standard does not exist, and talent
cannot be measured or considered a factor. A person may have
little talent for dancing in the traditional sense but become a
great dancer by changing the definition and limits of dance.

In general, talent, technique, and difficulty are easy to ap-
praise. There tends to be greater agreement in this kind of
judgment, and standards are more readily available from non-
art sources, making opinions based on these dimensions of a
work much safer from a social point of view. But attention paid
to these factors may only distract attention from the characteristics that make the work art. Ultimately, significance only derives from what is created, not from the technical accomplish-
ments of that creation.

If art does not exist merely "for its own sake" and the experience itself is not the only measure of its importance, then
significance depends upon what is referred to as "the relationship of art to reality." The meaning of the phrase depends entirely upon what is meant by "reality." Thus the questions or
problems of the significance of art and of the relationship of art
to life are, in general, relatively recent; perhaps they have become pressing only since the development of the avant-garde.
In the Renaissance, for example, the significance of art was
easily explained to everyone's satisfaction by its subject matter,
and even music developed "subject matter" through its religious
use and context. But meaning, reference, symbolism, and representation are not the only kinds of connections with reality.
Abstract art, by definition, has no relationship to the recognizable sensory patterns that we perceive as the real things of
the world, and yet it, too, is felt to be related to reality. It is
merely a slightly broader and less literal meaning of the word
"reality."

Music has always been basically a nonreferential art. Over

half a century ago—long before the current concern with the medium being the message—painting and sculpture became abstract. Now there is no art form that is representational throughout its entire spectrum. We are primarily concerned, therefore, with reality not as things and emotions but as principles and types. In other words, in discussing significance, we are primarily concerned with the significance of abstract or non-representational art.

Art, by definition, does not have a practical purpose. It is not created to accomplish a particular physical result. On the other hand, it may certainly have psychological and sociological implications and consequences. A tool is used to achieve a certain desired change in the state or condition of things; art is not a tool. But changes also occur without the use of tools and without the intent to make a change. Learning, for example, may be accomplished through teachers and teaching machines, but these are certainly not the only ways to learn. Thus art, even though it does not have a practical use, may cause changes.

The particular changes with which I am concerned are changes in the consciousness of man. Certainly the consciousness of man has changed. Its range, scope, and content have vastly increased. Cross-cultural comparisons give us an analogy for history and make this obvious: The consciousness of so-called primitive people may not be any better or worse than that of "civilized" man, but it is entirely different. History has produced changes in consciousness.

The important changes are those more or less permanent ones in the state and organization of consciousness. Any previously unknown thing in the perceptual field changes consciousness, but only the content of consciousness. Some things, however, may be of such a nature as to cause a reorganization of consciousness itself, of its expectancies, its values, and its functioning. In other words, most of experience may be integrated into consciousness without changing the character or nature of consciousness itself; some types of experience, on the other hand, can cause a complete change in the structure and efficiency of consciousness itself.

The alteration of consciousness is dramatically illustrated during sicknesses and in the effect of certain drugs. A feverish person or one who is "high" sees the world in an entirely different way. These changes are usually only temporary, however, and we are concerned here with those basic changes that occur when consciousness is forced against the things of this world, so to speak, rather than withdrawn from them.

The things of this world and the character of consciousness are interrelated. A thing or an action can force a reorganization of consciousness; a particular state of consciousness is necessary before a certain thing can be created or a certain action performed. Each may affect the other. Flying at 30,000 feet from New York to San Francisco in a few hours and watching the country move by as if it were a huge map forcefully presents to consciousness aspects of time and space that could only have been imagined a century ago. The invention of the airplane, on the other hand, depended upon knowledge that could only have been accumulated in a scientific-technological society and on aspects of consciousness not present in all cultures. The experience of flight causes changes in consciousness; flight was only possible because of changes in consciousness. This is only one example from many possible ones.

There is no question that extensive changes in the consciousness of man have taken place in the past and that consciousness will continue to change. There have been, and there will continue to be, concomitant changes in attitudes, beliefs, morals, social structure, and every other aspect of life, including art. This does not prove the causal relationship of art to these changes, however. From the whole cultural history of man it might theoretically be possible to remove all of art without affecting the rest in any way. Art might only follow and reflect changes that are due to other causes. There is no way to prove this.

It would seem unlikely, however, that changes in consciousness are not due, in part, to art. Art is vitally interrelated with the rest of culture, and the proposition that it can originate changes should not be too difficult to accept. One way of phrasing the problem, at least in analogy, might be to ask whether one sense modality has any effect on another. There is the common concept of each sense being localized in its own precise area of the brain, and this could be compared to the view that perceptions of art only affect other perceptions of art and not perceptions of the "real world." The effect of one sense on another is far from understood, but the model of discrete brain areas is not accepted as accurate at the most refined level. In *Subcortical Mechanisms of Behavior,* Robert A. McCleary and Robert Y. Moore write that "It seems best not to regard any one level of the brain as having sole control of particular behavioral functions, functions not shared or influenced to some extent by certain structures at other levels. . . . The brain is so reduntantly interlocked that it is difficult to know where a given subsystem begins or ends." * Thus we can believe that intersensory transfer takes place at some level. The way in which art changes the perception of life may not be understood, but it can be assumed that these changes take place.

Since changes in consciousness are psychological, they exist only in the individual. But when enough people develop similar states of consciousness, the change may be seen as cultural rather than personal. On a social-psychological level, an objectivity can be claimed for changes in consciousness. Thus we can establish an objective standard by which the significance of a work of art may be judged. A work of art can be seen as significant to the extent that it tends *to change basically the consciousness of man.*

As we have explained, if art is able to alter fundamentally the consciousness of man, it will indirectly produce changes in practical areas of life. This is not to suggest that a scientist looks at a painting and is so changed by the experience that he designs an experiment that he could not previously conceive. But, in time, it is *as if* this were true. Thus an artist may be seen as acting directly on the world.

But on an individual level, art seldom basically alters con-

* From *Subcortical Mechanisms of Behavior: The Psychological Functions of Primitive Parts* by Robert A. McCleary and Robert Y. Moore (New York: Basic Books, 1965).

sciousness instantaneously. I am not referring to those passing states that frequently continue to grip us after we leave a gallery, theatre, or concert hall, so that we briefly perceive the world in terms of art, but, as indicated before, to fundamental changes in the character or nature of consciousness that are not necessarily noticed by the individual. Perhaps a few people have been so drastically affected by a unitary experience of a work of art that their basic relationship to the data of reality has been changed. But just as the familiar "Eureka" experience of creativity or cases of sudden religious conversion, such as St. Paul's, can actually be seen to have a long, if unconscious, genesis in time, a work of art generally takes more than a moment to effect an alteration in individual consciousness. In certain cases the organization and dynamics of consciousness may be such that they may be quickly and easily changed, but change is more apt to be an extended process involving adjustments to new data and the elimination of conflicts and contradictions.

On a cultural level, it is even more apparent that alteration of consciousness is not an instantaneous phenomenon. The impact of any single work on society is not merely the sum total or average of all individual changes in consciousness that it causes. A work may also influence other works, thereby effecting additional changes. Or any alterations it does produce may be the basis for non-art creations that in turn cause further changes.

Thus there is a cultural diaspora or diffusion involved in the functional relationship between art and the rest of culture. In some cases, perhaps, little diffusion is necessary. The rate and duration of the assimilation are not constant. But in time, a work may become "translated" into other cultural modes of thought and perception. Art becomes philosophy; philosophy becomes political and scientific theory; politics and science change the mass entertainment industries, public utilities, and social structure.

At the same time, of course, changes at any of these other levels may also be forming consciousness in a way that will allow or predispose a previously impossible kind of art to be created. Social structure and philosophy are also becoming art.

This relationship between art and culture is elaborate and interwoven. Its processes are widespread and subtle. This means, for one thing, that the most apparent examples of the assimilation of art by society should not be taken as the only ones, as necessarily important, or as standards of measurement. One style of art, for example, is not more important than another merely because it is accepted more widely or has greater influence on popular culture. I am not suggesting a kind of public opinion poll in which those works that are the most popular or are taken up by design, fashion, entertainment fads, and so forth are declared the winners. In adopting art for its own mundane purposes, popular culture may take only those aspects of the art that have not required a basic change in consciousness. The most profound influences of art on life may be the least obvious.

Dispersion through the popular culture is one possible way for art to change consciousness, but it is not the best or only way. Art can also be disseminated, explained, and "translated" through the more specialized channels of higher education, theory, and philosophy, for example. Words may mirror a change in consciousness. Thought that is caused, provoked, based on, influenced, or made possible by an exposure to a work of art is one of the basic contacts of art with mundane reality and, ultimately, with significance.

One way to illustrate these relationships is to make an extended analogy between art and science. This does not mean that art and science can be equated in every respect. Obviously, there are fundamental differences. But certain important points about art may be illustrated by comparing it with science.

In the first place, both art and science are specialties. Neither is available at a very subtle level to a very large segment of the population. Everyone knows certain basic principles of chemistry or physics, of course, even if he has not had a specialized education and does not know the proper terminology. And anyone can look at a painting, listen to a piece of music, or attend a performance, and we can call the resulting experience an aesthetic one. But neither art nor science can be grasped to any extent without study and specialized involvement. The fine points of both may be experienced only by those with particular experience in the field.

In science this kind of specialization is taken for granted. We are not surprised when we cannot understand many of the words in a technical journal that has wide distribution within a particular field. A person who has not studied mathematics does not expect to understand an advanced formula. But many people think that art can be seen as well by the person with no specialized background as it can by the specialist. Art is deprecated as a coterie enterprise, while scientific collaborations are praised. It is frequently attacked as esoteric. Like the esoteric nature of science, it is necessary for art to exist on this level, however, in order to achieve significance. In our terms, entertainment, decoration, and beauty may be for the mass audience, but art is not. Like the scientist, the avant-garde artist is working for a very limited audience whose experience, understanding of historical developments and current concepts in the field, and interest make it possible for it to appreciate points that are unavailable to a general audience.

In science certain current and pressing problems are widely recognized. Many medical research people are trying to find a cure for cancer. Many others all over the world are perfecting heart transplants. Although it is possible that individual scientists may be working alone in entirely unique areas, there is a tendency in science for many people to be involved simultaneously on the same problem. The theory of natural selection was formulated independently at the same time by both Charles Darwin and Alfred Russell Wallace.

I believe that the same is true in art. Certain problems are widely felt. Even when isolated from each other's work, artists may develop in the same direction. At each moment in history certain possibilities exist and others have been closed off.

All scientists are not involved with adding to the total of

man's knowledge. Some teach, promulgating the knowledge that already exists. Others work in areas such as quality control where scientific techniques are necessary. In the same way, not all artists are concerned with the new. Many are satisfied to work in accepted styles and manners. But in art as in science, it is the new that gives the field its significance. The scientific meaning of the word "experiment" does not fit artistic creation with any precision, but it accurately indicates the ambition of some artists to investigate new areas of experience.

The dispersion of art into the culture that was mentioned before may also be clarified by analogy with science. Scientific discoveries exist at a theoretical level that can be understood only by a relatively small number of specialists. In part, these discoveries suggest other theoretical research and remain, so to speak, within the area of science. But they are also simplified and explained so that a broader public can understand them. They may cause modifications in existing products or methods. Their practical implications may bring about the invention of many new tools and techniques that were previously impossible. A purely theoretical discovery may have a wide impact on culture even though it, in itself, is never perceived or understood by the general public. The "translation" of art into life occurs in an analogous manner.

From this point of view, abstract art is not "dehumanized," as many have said. It lacks humanity no more than scientific research does. Abstraction can be seen as a specialized language that has an abundance of intra-art contrast elements. It is perceived primarily in terms of other art in the manner discussed previously. This does not mean that representational art is not seen in the historical context. All art is abstract to a certain extent, and representation has its own aesthetic history. But representational art, by definition, allows certain direct comparisons with the world that can be made outside of the cultural-historical context of art. The terminology is, to this extent, available to a wider audience.

Scientific research can have two kinds of significance. It can be provocative and suggestive, even if incorrect, and thus lead to further investigations. Or it can be the basis for new developments in the practical world. As has been suggested, this is analogous to the significance of art. The power of certain works to alter consciousness may be severely limited by their particular context. They may only influence artists and not be seen as significant except by a limited number of people. Other works are able to influence culture in a more diffuse way and on a wider level, perhaps fundamentally altering the consciousness of man.

Thus the word "significance" has been used in two different ways: as a psychological concept and on the social-psychological level. On the social level, significance can have a kind of objectivity. Shakespeare and Picasso are great, whether or not I care for them. The reasons are as much a part of the work as any other element. The work cannot be separated from its historical context. Of course this is a limited kind of objectivity. The historical context is not absolutely fixed, and a degree of change is involved. On the other hand, it is not unstable.

The connection between the two kinds of significance, the subjective and the objective, lies in the method of validating the art experience. This whole concept is hypothetical. It is based on the feeling and assumption that art somehow is useful practically to the individual. As we have discussed before, this does not mean that it functions in the world as a tool to achieve certain ends. But art can be seen as a psychological tool. In this sense, it is used in order better to understand the nature of reality. This occurs on an integrative unconscious level. I do not mean that only we understand information about reality, but that we are able to understand more of its organization and basic structure. From this point of view, changes in individual consciousness allow more information to enter, but they are not necessarily caused by information as such.

If we better understand the nature of reality, we should be able to function better. I believe that this is true. As I see it, art enables us to live more "accurately" and, therefore, more successfully. But there is no way to prove this. We cannot, in the same way, objectively prove the accuracy of religious beliefs, although they engender similar feelings of truth and usefulness. In this sense, all art is religious. Or, in philosophical terms, it is metaphysical. The usefulness of truth and the danger of using false information also explains why "good" art is seen as being moral and "bad" art as immoral.

On the psychological level, each person validates or "checks out" the usefulness of art for himself. What is useful for one person is not necessarily useful for another. This is especially true because we function in culture. Much of the usefulness of art may be "only" social and cultural.

Thus the relationship between perceived significance on an individual level and our objective sociopsychological significance exists in two entirely different modes. One of these modes could be called the retrospective. With the perspective of time, the various interrelationships of art with the other aspects of culture become clear. Michaelangelo is great in an objective sense. In all likelihood, greatness will also be perceived as a quality of his work. Among other particular negative psychological factors, there might be a reaction against his fame, but his work is more apt to be seen positively because of "reinforcements" from later cultural developments. In retrospect Michaelangelo's art is justified and supported by its influence on ethical and philosophical as well as iconographic areas. Whether or not the observer knows Michaelangelo's name or has studied art history is not the vital point. The influence of a work of art on culture tends to create and assure its own appreciation. It will "check out" in many different ways.

The second way in which significance can be experienced as an attribute of a work of art could be called the hypothetical mode. It involves estimates about the future rather than judgments about the past. A work that has just been created cannot be put into the same kind of historical context that an older work can. It may be related to art and non-art sources in the culture, but the impact of the work on culture and consciousness cannot be appraised objectively. The work, of course, will not yet have been able to create its own context of appreciation. But the future of the work may, in a sense, be estimated. The potential of a work to influence culture and change certain aspects of consciousness may become a hypothetical dimension of the aesthetic experience.

Changes in culture emphasize the difficulty and the pertinence of the historical mode. If the future is expected to be exactly like the past, all judgments become "retrospective" even when they are made about the future. On the other hand, a changing culture means that the character and nature of prevalent tendencies must be understood in order to make accurate estimates about the future. These tendencies, of course, derive from the past, but as the cultural rate of change increases, their origin and genesis tend to grow closer to the present moment. The history that is vital is very recent history.

This suggests that avant-garde art would not be recognizable as such if accelerating cultural change had not increased its visibility. Artists have always been concerned with the future. The hypothetical mode has always been pertinent. But there has not always been much difference between retrospective and hypothetical judgments. The concern for the directionality of art that defines the avant-garde becomes magnified by rapid cultural change.

Strangely enough, change seems to be understood by the youthful better than by the elderly. Perhaps it is because the older people tend to explain change in terms of the past, while the young, looking with naïve need, see the unique character and qualities of the transition. At any rate, there is a close identification between the avant-garde and youthful attitudes of self-actualization and learning.

6 | Thus we have a view of art that does not rely on a subjective aesthetic attitude or state. This view proposes that the way in which art is perceived is basically the same as the way in which the world is perceived, and that a change in one can bring about a change in the other. The various sense modalities are seen as unified at a deep level where there is an exchange between them. Therefore, even though consciousness precedes perception, certain perceptions are able to change the limits or

basic character of consciousness itself. It is upon these changes that the significance of art depends.

Knowledge determines, in part, the nature of experience. Like a person whose eyes are not yet fully adapted to the light, we can see only what the specific conditions and content of our consciousness allow us to see. And since the consciousness of man changes, the work of art created now will not be experienced in the same way in the future anymore than we can experience the art of the past just as it was when it was first produced. From this point of view, all art is mental rather than physical. Of course this makes the aesthetic experience subjective and relativistic, but it would require an absolute, godlike omniscience to be aware of all the factors that could contribute to the experience of any work and to make the manifold experiences of all men objective.

It was suggested, however, that history gives a kind of cultural objectivity to the significance of art. This same kind of objectivity cannot be obtained in the present, and the perception and evaluation of contemporary art must exist in a different, hypothetical, mode.

Since the perception of all aesthetic elements, including the new, varies from person to person, it is important to stress the aspect of specialization. The understanding of art by artists and by others who spend their lives involved with art has somewhat more importance, in these terms, than the average or usual reaction. Art, as we have been concerned with it here, can be more subtle and demanding than the so-called popular arts.

Because of their emphasis upon the sociopsychological context of perception, these views of art could be called "situational aesthetics." Because of a simultaneous emphasis upon history and the influence of time, they could be called "historical aesthetics." They were given impetus by a desire to explain the attitude of the avant-garde that "A work of art that is created today is not good because it is new, but it cannot be significant unless it is new."

If the aesthetic emphasis is primarily on the mental state

engendered by certain creations of man, there are no physical or technical limitations on what can be art. There are no rules that theatre must use words, that paintings must be illusionistic or non-illusionistic, that music must be harmonic, and so forth. Anything that an artist presents as having experiential significance is considered art.

Naturalistic
Theatre

There is no question about the greatness of naturalism as a dramatic form. Officially initiated by Zola's Preface to *Thérèse Raquin* in 1873, it spread throughout Europe before the turn of the century and now forms an important part of the dramatic literature of every major country in the world. Several of its playwrights, such as Ibsen, Strindberg, and Chekov—I am more concerned here with the possible naturalism of production and am not quibbling over the exact literary limits of naturalism— are, by common agreement, among the most significant in the history of theatre. For almost a century, this form of drama has been a powerful force operating upon human attitudes and ideas. Naturalism has played a dominant part in forming the consciousness of our time.

And yet, when we see a naturalistic production today of a play by Ibsen or Strindberg, for example, we do not experience it as it was originally experienced. This difference does not depend entirely on the fact that it is quite a different production. All art, not only that of the theatre, suffers from an inability, so to speak, to be experienced forever in exactly the same way it was when it was produced. A major part of the unique personal experience of art depends upon cultural-historical factors; the work is perceived in terms of its immediate context. Time passes, and the context changes, even if the physical work itself does not. Thus we cannot actually experience the paintings of Courbet or Millet, for example (I pick works that have some theoretical and stylistic similarity to naturalistic theatre), in the same way that a person in the nineteenth century did. Time has changed our way of perceiving, even though the stimuli are unchanged. In writing *Thérèse Raquin*, Zola was influenced by Claud Bernard's *An Introduction to the Study of Experimental Medicine* and not by Freud; Freud was 17 years old when the play was first produced, and if, hypothetically, we could step into a theatre and see that original performance just as we can see the original Courbets and Millets in a museum, we could not eradicate the tremendous formative effect that Freud's ideas, to take only one major aspect of the historical differential, have had on our minds. We could not actually experience that original production as if Freudian theory and all the myriad other intervening changes in man's consciousness did not exist.

Thus, what is *perceived* as naturalistic in one time is not necessarily perceived as naturalistic in another. The theoretical naturalistic standard of absolute verisimilitude has remained unchanged, but its application has varied through recent history, and we will no longer accept that which was once considered to be absolutely convincing. Although the motion picture camera was not perfected until long after the rise of naturalism, the changes in what has been considered to be naturalistic acting, for example, may be seen in old films, where we may assume that a high degree of correlation existed between acting in motion pictures and on the stage. If we could, miraculously, be present with our contemporary consciousness at one of the original performances of, say, Ibsen or Strindberg, we would find the actors quite "inaccurate" in their reproduction of reality. (Although the Stanislavsky "method" is too often given credit, for example, as being the first thorough, systematic, and scientific analysis of acting techniques, it was preceded by the Delsarte system, the basis of what we consider the height of melodramatic acting. Delsarte spent many years intensively studying and categorizing the variety of physical responses to emotion. His rules for poses and strictly defined movements were based on careful investigation and analysis; the rigorous, empirical and scientific nature of his system is one of the things that made it appealing to the naturalistically inclined theatre people of his time.)

A distinction may therefore be made between contemporary plays written and produced in the naturalistic style and current naturalistic productions of plays by historically important playwrights such as Ibsen, Strindberg, and Chekov. In looking at the historical play, whatever we know of its total context in time becomes part of the perception. A theatrically informed and sophisticated person does not see it as if it had been written by a contemporary. Although much of the process is unconscious, we imaginatively reconstruct, so to speak, the experience of the original spectator and sense the relationship of the work to its own time; we are also made aware of the changes that have occurred in our perception and the influence that the play has had on our own time. The complete historical perception is complex, pervasive, and powerful. And it is quite different in many respects from the perception of the contemporary play.

The question of the viability of naturalism in our time can, therefore, be understood as applying differently to historical playwrights and to contemporary ones. Since a production is not preserved in a museum the way a painting is, the historically important plays (including, if possible, accurate recreations of significant productions based on lesser-known scripts) must be produced. This is vital to our understanding. But it is not the same thing as saying that naturalism has any aesthetic validity as a contemporary art form. The Courbets and Millets are of significance, and we would not burn them, but contemporary painters no longer work in that style. The fact that naturalism has had no importance for painting and sculpture for at least 75 years does not, of course, prove that theatrical naturalism has no validity for our time. For one thing, theatre has usually followed the other arts rather than influenced them. But the great importance of the reproductions of historical naturalistic plays does not aesthetically justify contemporary plays created in the historical naturalistic form, a form whose clearly defined limits and conventions were established in another era. This kind of naturalism is an anachronism that faces certain problems in our time.

In the present day, naturalism may be considered, sociologically, in terms of its impact on various audiences. At one extreme, literal correspondence with physical, perceptual reality is the only aesthetic standard of a large, artistically naïve segment of the population. Other standards, such as "I like it" and "It's fun," may be used for song and dance and broad comedy but a common unsophisticated standard of drama is "It's so real." For this audience, naturalism will always have an importance. But, although many theatre practitioners are not aware of the fact, a large audience does not turn entertainment into art. Sophistication is no better (or worse) than naïveté, and there is no reason why anyone or everyone should be interested in art, but I prefer to discuss naturalism as it relates to the art of theatre. The audience for art is a limited one. For one thing, it has an awareness of theatrical possibilities that the popular mass audience does not have. Its knowledge of classicism, romanticism, neoclassicism, and other forms that preceded naturalism as well as those forms that postdate the birth of naturalism such as expressionism, surrealism, and the modernization of surrealism called Theatre of the Absurd, gives it an entirely different perception of the theatrical presentation. The problems of naturalism in our time exist in this specific cultural context: The traditional shape of naturalistic drama transmitted from the past is no longer aesthetically viable.

In the Preface to *Miss Julie,* Strindberg wrote, "We have so much else on stage that is conventional, and in which we are asked to believe, that we might at least be spared the too great effort of believing in painted pans and kettles." On the other hand, Vsevolod Meyerhold wrote in *On the Theatre* that "The trees used in the naturalistic theatre seem crude, unnatural, and much more artificial in their three-dimensions than painted, two-dimensional trees." I do not intend in this discussion to take sides with either of these men and argue whether the premises of naturalism are "right" or "wrong." Understanding does not require value judgments. "Right" and "wrong" in art are personal decisions, correct only for the person. Strindberg, at the moment he wrote, was for greater naturalism; Meyerhold was opposed to literalness in staging. Each was "right" for himself. Both were "right" for history. Their statements tell us more about the men and their historical positions than they do about naturalism. The work of both men added to the consciousness of man, and what each has done does not need to be destroyed or depreciated—nothing needs to be removed, so to speak, from the consciousness they have created—so that the other's work may have value.

Any criticism of naturalism must make allowances for its temporal position and should be in terms of its own "rules," goals, and system of values. There would be little point, for example, in stating that I think that even in the most absolute manifestations of historical naturalism there is still too much "on stage that is conventional, and in which we are asked to believe, and that we might . . . be spared the too great effort . . ." or in discussing my personal negative attitudes toward storytelling and fantasy, projection and empathy, mood and characterization, and so forth. These are all elements of the naturalistic form itself. To analyze and describe naturalism and then label each of the elements pejoratively would serve no function. No art form has universal appeal, and we could expect a certain amount of people to be unresponsive to, or disinterested in, naturalism. On the other hand, the goals and ideas of naturalism are clear and widely understood; it is in terms of these values that the problems of naturalism in our own times should be evaluated.

Naturalistic theatre attempts to present an exact copy of life to the senses. It approximates this goal as closely as it is able. This does not, of course, mean that the spectator is deluded into believing that the occurrences acted on stage are actually taking place. No form of drama is absolutely illusionistic. Even the most convincing details of naturalistic production and elements of true verisimilitude such as Antoine's real sides of beef and Belasco's faucets from which real water flowed must always exist in a context of pretense. Dramatic naturalism in its most rigorous form cannot eliminate all convention.

This is not true of motion pictures. Motion pictures can be completely naturalistic; drama cannot. The film, as a medium, is always real. It has intrinsic fidelity to the physical world, recording exactly what is there. Any angle of view, foreshortening, or effect is believed no matter how unusual and unlike life. Plays, by definition, are make-believe, while the camera is a tool for recording whatever reality is presented to it. This means that a play that is filmed gains in the process a kind of reality that it did not have on the stage. The pretense is one step further away, so to speak, filtered through the reality of the medium. This filtering process gives a certain, perhaps slight, naturalistic *quality* to all film experience. This quality is apparent, for example, even in abstract and animated films in the tendency to ponder on what it "really is" and to examine how the perceived image was created.

One of the historic concerns of the naturalistic theatre was the relationship of the human being to his social and physical environment. This concern is better served by motion pictures. The camera can provide absolutely naturalistic backgrounds and settings for actors, and its flexibility allows it to register scenes that could not be physically reproduced on any stage because of their scale and scope. Closeups can focus magni-

fied details and textures that the audience-performance relationship established by an illusionistic stage does not allow.

The acting element can also be more naturalistic in filmed
drama. While anyone on stage, merely because of his awareness of the audience situation, for one thing, remains outside
of the imaginary context in which he is placed, hidden cameras
may turn passersby and crowds, for example, into "actors" in
a story. This "acting" is truly naturalistic. Actual acting can
also be more naturalistic on films than it can be on stage. Since
the information already given in the story, the camera, other
elements and actors in a scene, and the editing may often do
the acting *for* a performer, so to speak, acting technique is
not always needed in films. The borderline between actual
documentary and storytelling dramatic films has been blurred
by *cinéma vérité* and the use of "found" non-professional
actors in real locales. The stage, with its stringent requirements of visual and vocal projection, does not permit an in-
experienced person "borrowed" from life to appear natural.
Films, on the other hand, project the smallest detail of in-
stinctive gesture or expression; "stage whispers" and other
physical adjustments are not necessary, and the energy employed may be the same as in everyday life.

Nor is the subject matter of documentary films less dramatic
than that of the stage. We see soldiers actually die; people
are swept away in a flood or killed in an accident. There is a
kind of ultimate naturalism in the continuing and repeatable
recording of their deaths. The crucial, tense moments of a
sporting event, the suspense and humor of "human interest"
stories, all the "theatrics" of life are preserved with im-
mediacy and directness. If an artist is profoundly interested
in naturalism as a form of drama, there is no reason why he
should want or need the stage.

An awareness of editing techniques (and such unedited
films as Andy Warhol's *Empire*, an eight hour motion picture
of the Empire State Building in which the camera remains
motionless) makes clearer to us the way naturalistic plays
actually manipulate and arrange entrances, exits, and scene

structure. Since the camera is "invisible" it does not draw attention to conventions of frontality as powerfully as does a proscenium stage. And lighting in motion pictures can be much more naturalistic than that of the stage. The only really naturalistic stage lighting that I have ever seen was in small theatres that could not afford better, and where the action could be seen, for example, by the light of a single bulb. Usually, when a candle is lighted or a switch flipped, hidden spotlights provide the "naturalistic" light in at least two different colors.

It is perhaps an oversimplification to say that the development of the still photograph made it no longer necessary to paint illusionistic paintings. But it is as if this were true. In the same way, the development of the motion picture has radically altered our standards of dramatic naturalism. It has changed practical limits and theoretical aspirations as well as our basic perceptions, expectancies, and attitudes. The necessary and unavoidable conventions and artifices of the stage stand out with greater clarity in comparison with a medium that can, by its nature, be absolutely naturalistic. Without questioning the goals of naturalism, it has become apparent that they can, like the more obvious ones of illusionistic painting, be better achieved in a newer medium.

It is not necessary, however, to find the problems with historical naturalism in our time only in contrast to film. Within the drama itself, the goals of naturalism are being achieved in nontraditional ways. In 1967 *A Study in Habitation* (also called *Life with the Family*) was staged by Jerry Shultz at an off off-Broadway theatre in New York. The concept was quite simple: to have a group of people actually live together as a family, cooking, eating, and sleeping on a stage furnished like an apartment for twenty-four hours a day over an indefinite period of time. The family was not a real one, but was composed of people "playing" the various "members"; "visitors" to the "home" were numerous. Spectators paid admission and watched as much of the "endless" performance as they wished. The failures of the presentation—its inability to achieve its implicit goals—are less important in terms of our discussion than the goals themselves, which were basically naturalistic. Among other things, historical naturalism established a more functional relationship between actor and the setting or décor: Rather than playing against a background, the performer was enclosed in a box set and surrounded by a multitude of props that he could actually touch and use. A *Study in Habitation* attempted to develop this concept further than the naturalists had done. If people are actually living on the stage, their relationship to the physical environment should eventually be more subtle, symbiotic, and naturalistic than if they only spent part of the rehearsal and performance there. The setting would be created, to a good extent, by the performers themselves, as it generally is in real life, rather than by a designer. And since real life has no act curtains and intermissions, the performance was continuous. Basically, A *Study in Habitation* was an attempt to present "fourth wall" naturalistic drama with all its voyeuristic implications in a way that would actually seem natural in our age.

While improvisation, as used in A *Study in Habitation*, attempts to do away with, among other things, even the unconscious consistencies of verbal style, attitude, and mannerism that mark literary dialogue, some playwrights have attempted to achieve greater naturalism and authenticity by using words as they actually were spoken on particular occasions. Shaw and Anouilh may have incorporated lines from the transcript of the trial of Joan of Arc into their plays about the saint primarily because they had poetic and literary qualities in themselves, but all of the speeches in Peter Weiss's *The Investigation* were taken verbatim from the transcript of a war crimes trial. Weiss edited the material, but he did not write any dialogue; since this is known by the audience, the play is more naturalistic in quality and impact than he could otherwise have made it. *In the Matter of J. Robert Oppenheimer*, by Heinar Kipphardt, attempts to exploit the powers of both literal documentary and more traditional forms: based on a hearing by the Atomic Energy Commission, the play leaves it up to the spectator whether particular speeches were invented or were taken from the transcript. This blending of fact and fiction caused several of the hearing's participants, including Dr. Oppenheimer, to protest.

Although perhaps not recognizable as such when compared to traditional "fourth wall" naturalism, the naturalistic ideal was one essential aspect of my own *Room 706* (see "Performance Chronology," p. 183). An impromptu discussion among three people was filmed and recorded, and this brief "slice of life" was reenacted during the performance by the people themselves as well as by other actors. One assumption was that verbal material taken directly from life should be more natural than anything a playwright could produce: With all of its hesitations, unfinished sentences, interruptions, "vocalized thinking," and other imperfections, the unedited record might not be as clear, well-structured, informative, or interesting as synthetic dialogue, but it and the imitated, rather than invented, movements would have the basic quality of verisimilitude. Another assumption was that even within the limitations of fixed dialogue and movements—within the restrictions of traditional acting, in other words—a person impersonating himself should be able to get closer, in a certain sense, to absolute naturalism than would be possible in any other way.

Contemporary performances such as the ones I have mentioned, not only continue and develop the naturalistic impulse, they attempt to recapture that aspect of historical naturalism that, even when viewing an accurate "museum" production that re-creates a historical work as closely as possible, can now only be imaginatively understood rather than directly perceived. At the height of its importance, naturalism gained power not from the fact that it was completely illusionistic but because it had greater verisimilitude than preceding forms. In other words, it benefited from a contrast and comparison with earlier forms of theatre: It commented upon them, so to speak, and this comment was part of its content. Contemporary naturalistic productions do not have this potential. Only by breaking the form—by becoming more naturalistic than naturalism—can they exploit it.

Naturalism, then, can be seen in our time as a fixed and

conventionalized form of theatre that does not explicitly admit its conventions and claims to be as close to real life as possible, while actually falling short of this goal because of its self-imposed limitations. These limitations have been clarified, in part, by certain contemporary productions that preserve the ideal spirit of naturalism, even though they take significantly different forms. Granting that all forms of drama are necessarily unreal, naturalism, as history has given it to us, is no longer the most naturalistic of possible theatre experience. If the ideals and ambitions of historical naturalism are still viable, the forms they must take are quite different from the form we know as "naturalism."

INTERMEDIA

Richard Schechner, the editor of what was then the *Tulane Drama Review*, and I drove up to interview John Cage for the special issue of *TDR* that I was putting together on Happenings and other new forms of theatre. Richard asked Cage what he thought of the work of Bertold Brecht and Jean Genet. Cage's answer is not in the published interview. He said that he was not familiar with Genet and described his reactions to a performance he had seen of a Brecht play by the Berliner Ensemble.

As soon as we left, Richard expressed his amazement that Cage did not know Genet's work. He apparently felt that anyone deeply involved in one art could be expected to know the major practitioners of other arts. I knew it was not true. The arts still tend to be specialties. I was thinking of our arrival, when Cage introduced us to two friends who were visiting him. The name of one was Jasper Johns. "Are you an artist?" Richard asked, and began talking about the summer he had spent directing at a theatre in Provincetown, the traditional artists' colony.

The
New
Theatre

Since the turn of the century, most art forms have vastly expanded their materials and scope. Totally abstract or non-objective painting and sculpture, unheard of in 1900, is practiced by many major artists today. Composers tend to discard traditional Western scales and harmonies, and atonal music is relatively common. Poetry has abandoned rhyme, meter, and syntax. Almost alone among the arts, theatre has lagged. But during the last few years there have been a number of performances that begin to bring theatre into some relation with the other arts. These works, as well as productions in other performance-oriented fields, force us to examine theatre in a new light and raise questions about the meaning of the word "theatre" itself.

In discussing this new theatre, new terms are needed. A few have already been provided by public usage, although they need clarification and standardization. Others will have to be created. Accurate nomenclature is important—not for the sake of limitation but to facilitate easy, accurate, and creative exchange among those concerned with the work and its concepts.

It is clear, however, that perfect definitions are almost impossible to derive from actual recent theatrical productions. Just as no *formal* distinctions between poetry and prose can be made in some cases, and passages of "prose" are published in anthologies of "poetry," and as traditional categories of "painting" and "sculpture" grow less and less applicable to much modern work, so theatre exists not as an entity but as a continuum blending into other arts. Each name and term refers only to a significant point on this continuum. Definitions apply to *central tendency,* but cannot set precise limits.

For example, we find that theatre blends at one extreme into painting and sculpture. Traditionally these arts did not structure the time dimension as theatre does, but in recent years paintings and sculptures have begun to move and give off sound. They have become "performers." Some of the works of Rauschenberg and Tinguely are obvious examples, and pieces of kinetic sculpture by Len Lye have been exhibited to an audience from the stage in New York's Museum of Modern Art. Art displays, such as the large Surrealist exhibitions and the recent "labyrinths" of the Groupe de Recherche d'Art Visuel de Paris, are turned into environmental mazes through which the spectator wanders, creating a loose time structure. The Environment which completely surrounds the viewer has become an accepted art form.

Although almost all Environments have made use of light, sound, and movement, *Eat* by Allan Kaprow went one step further by employing human beings as the "mechanized" elements. The people involved functioned within narrow and well-defined limits of behavior. Their tasks, which had no development or progression, were repeated without variation. They responded only to particular actions on the part of the spectators—only when their "switch was turned on." It may be easy to keep "performing" paintings and sculptures within the categories of those arts, but does Kaprow's use of the human performer make his *Eat* "theatre"? Certainly *Eat* is at the dividing line between forms. My own opinion is that the very strong emphasis upon static environmental elements outweighs the performance elements. *Eat* is not quite theatre. It is just this kind of weighing, this evaluation guided by dominant characteristics and central tendency, which must be used in assigning works of the new theatre to a category.

The most convenient beginning for a discussion of the new theatre is John Cage. Cage's thought, in his teaching, writing, lectures, and works, is the backbone of the new theatre. In the first place, Cage refuses as a composer to accept any limits for music. Traditional sound producers did not satisfy him, and he created his own instruments: the prepared piano, in which various materials were placed on the strings of a piano to change the qualities of the sounds; the water gong, which was lowered into water while vibrating to produce a change in tone; and so forth. Not only did he equate sound and silence so that long passages of silence were integral parts of his compositions, but he pointed out that absolute silence does not exist. (He is fond of describing his experience in a theoretically soundproof research room in which he heard two sounds: the circulation of his blood and the functioning of his nervous system.) If sound is ever present, so are the other senses, and Cage has gone so far as to deny the existence of music itself, if music is considered as hearing isolated from sight, touch, smell, etc.

These considerations led to a shift of emphasis in Cage's concerts toward non-auditory elements. Of course the performance of music for an audience is never entirely auditory. Rituals of tuning up, the appearance of the conductor, and the attitudes, behavior, and dress of the musicians are important parts of the experience. Although we enjoy watching performances on traditional instruments (at a piano recital, for example, seats on the keyboard side are preferred), the visual aspects are relatively easy to take for granted (and those who cannot see the keyboard do not feel cheated). A new instrument, such as a water gong, or a new way of playing, such as reaching inside the piano to pluck the strings, calls attention to itself: *how* the sound is produced becomes as significant a part of the experience as the *quality* of the sound itself. This theatricalization of a musical performance exists on an entirely different level from the emotional dramatizations of a Bernstein.

If any kind of sound producer may be used to make music, and if silence is also music (because true silence does not exist), it follows that any activity or event may be presented as part of a music concert. La Monte Young may use a butterfly as his sound source; the ONCE group can refer to the performance of a piece which includes the broadcast narration of a horse race (the only primarily auditory element), the projected image of rolling marbles, and a series of people moving in various ways (on roller skates, etc.) as "music."

This emphasis upon performance, which is one result of a refusal to place limits upon music, draws attention to the performer himself. But the musician is not acting. Acting might be defined as the creation of character and/or place: details of "who" and "where" the performer is are necessary to the performance. The actor functions within subjective or objective person-place matrices. The musician, on the other hand, is *non-matrixed*. He attempts to be no one other than himself, nor does he function in a place other than that which physically contains him and the audience.

Non-matrixed performances are not uncommon. Although the audience-performer relationship which is the basis of theatre exists in sporting events, for example, the athlete does not create character or place. Nor is such imaginary information a part of the half-time spectacle of a football game, religious or secular rituals, political conventions, or many other activities in "real life." The tendency, however, is to deny the performers in these situations serious consideration either because, like the musician, they are not a "legitimate" and accepted part of the formal experience, or because the works in which they appear are not art. My point is not to change our view of these "common" events but to suggest the profound possibilities and potentialities of non-matrixed performing for the theatre.

Since acting is, by definition, matrixed performing, why not simply use the terms "acting" and "non-acting" rather than suggesting new and fairly awkward terms? The fact is that "non-acting" would be equally awkward and less meaningful. Matrix is a larger and more inclusive concept than the activity of the performer, and a person may be matrixed without acting. Acting is something that a performer does; matrix can be externally imposed upon his behavior. The context of place, for example, as determined by the physical setting and the information provided verbally and visually by the production, is frequently so strong that it makes an "actor" out of any person, such as an extra, who walks upon the stage. In many cases nothing needs to be done in order to "act." The priest in church performing part of the service, the football player warming-up and playing the game, the sign painter being raised on a scaffold while passersby watch, are not matrixed by character or place. Even their specific, identifying clothing does not make them "characters." Yet the same people might do exactly the same things in a play involving a scene of worship, a football game, or the creation of a large sign, and become "actors" because of the context.[1]

This does not mean that there is always a clear line between matrixed and non-matrixed performing. The terms refer to polar conceptions which are quite obvious in their pure forms, but a continuum exists between them, and it is possible that this or that performance might be difficult to categorize. In

[1] Of course the behavior in "real life" and on stage might not be exactly the same. A particular emotional reaction to facing an audience in the theatre situation could be expected. But while *created* or acted emotions are part of character matrix, *real* emotions are not. The question of emotion will be touched on again below.

other words, the strength of character-place matrices may be described as "strong" or "weak" and the exact point at which a weak matrix becomes non-matrix is not easy to perceive. But even in the extreme case in which both the work of the performer and the information provided by his context are so vague and nonspecific that we could not explain "who" he was or "where" he was supposed to be, we often feel that he is someone other than himself or in some place other than the actual place of performance. We know when we are suspending disbelief or being asked to suspend it.

Non-matrixed performances which are complete in themselves are referred to as Events. A piano is destroyed. The orchestra conductor walks on stage, bows to the audience, raises his baton, and the curtain falls. A formally dressed man appears with a French horn under his arm; when he bows, ball bearings pour from the bell of the horn in a noisy cascade. A person asks if La Monte Young is in the audience; when there is no answer, he leaves. A man sets a balloon on stage, carefully estimates the distance as he walks away from it, then does a backward flip, landing on the balloon and breaking it. Since Events are usually short, they are frequently performed as parts of longer programs. The Fluxus group, a fairly loose organization which includes most of the people working in the form in New York, has presented many "concerts" composed entirely of Events. The form demonstrates a type of performing that is widely used in the new theatre and which is one of its most important contributions.

In his music Cage abandoned harmony, the traditional means of structuring a composition, and replaced it with duration. This was logically consistent, since duration was the only dimension of music which applied to silence as well as to sounds. Duration could also be used to structure spoken material, and Cage built lectures with these same techniques. Indeed, duration is the one dimension which exists in *all* performance, and in the summer of 1952, stimulated no doubt by his awareness of the performance aspects of music and by his programmatic refusal to place limits upon the sounds used or the manner in which they were produced, Cage presented a work at Black Mountain College which combined dance, motion pictures, poetry and prose readings, and recorded music. These materials were handled exactly as if they had been sounds. The musical and non-musical elements were all precisely scored for points of entry into the piece and duration— a wide variety of performance materials was "orchestrated."

Theatre as we have generally known it is based primarily upon *information structure*. Not only do the individual elements of a presentation generate meaning, but each conveys meaning to and receives it from the other elements. This was not true of the piece which Cage presented at Black Mountain College. Although some of the elements contained information, the performance units did not pass information back and forth or "explain" each other. The film, for example, which was of the cook at the school and later of a sunset, did not help the spectator to "understand" the dance any more clearly than if the dance had been presented by itself. The ideas expressed in the poetry had no intentional relationship to the ideas contained in the prose. The elements remained intellectually discrete. Each was a separate compartment. The structure was *alogical*.

The information structure of traditional theatre is not alogical but either logical or illogical. Information is built and interrelated in both the logical well-made play and the "illogical" dream, surreal, or absurd play. Illogic depends upon an awareness of what is logical. Alogical structure stands completely outside of these relationships.

Of course the structure of all music (overlooking the "waterfalls" and "twittering birds" of program music and the written program itself, which adds its own information structure to the composition) and of abstract or nonobjective painting and sculpture is alogical. It depends upon sensory rather than intellectual relationships. Literature, on the other hand, depends primarily upon information structure. It is this fact rather than a reliance upon written script material or the use of words which makes it so easy and so correct to call traditional theatre "*literary* theatre." As Cage's piece demonstrated, "verbal" should not be confused with "literary." Nor is the nonverbal necessarily alogical. Information is conveyed by movement, setting, and lighting as well as by words, and a mime play, although more limited in its technical means, constructs the same web of information that a dialogue play does. Both are literary. The spectator "reads" the performance.[2]

A performance using a variety of materials (films, dance, readings, music, etc.) in a compartmented structure, and making use of essentially non-matrixed performance, is a Happening. Thus the distinction between Happenings and Events can be made on the basis of compartments or logically discrete elements. The Event is limited to one compartment, while the Happening contains several, most often sequential, compartments, and a variety of primary materials.

The name "Happening" was taken by the public from *18 Happenings in 6 Parts* by Allan Kaprow (who had studied with Cage), which was presented in 1959. Since then it has been applied indiscriminately to many performances ranging from plays to parlor games. It has been a fad word, although the small attendance at presentations prevents Happenings themselves from being called a fad. Nobody seems to like the word except the public. Since the name was first applied to a piece by Kaprow, it tends to be his word, and some other artists, not caring for the slightest implication that their work is not at least 100% original, do not publicly apply the name "Happening" to their productions. (I am reminded of the person who said he did not want to go to a particular Happening

_____

[2] Thus it is not essentially the degree of correlation between the written script and the performance which makes a theatre piece "literary." Whether or not it began from written material, any production, no matter how alogical, may be described in words, and the description could then be used as the literary basis for another production. On the other hand, there is the additional question of the latitude of interpretation allowed by a printed script—e.g., George Brecht's *Exit*, the "score" of which consists in its entirety of the single word with no directions or suggestions for interpretation and realization. *Any* written material, and even nonverbal material, may serve as the "script" for a performance.

because he had seen a Happening already. It was as if he were saying that he did not want to read a particular novel because he had read a novel once.) Names are beginning to proliferate: Theatre Piece (Robert Whitman), Action Theatre (Ken Dewey), Ray Gun Theatre (Claes Oldenburg), Kinetic Theatre (Carolee Schneemann), etc. The ONCE group and Ann Halprin perform works which I would call Happenings, but they refer to them as "music," "dance," or by no generic name. Because nothing better has been coined to replace it, I will use the term "Happening."

A dominant aspect of Cage's thought has been his concern with the environmental or directional aspects of performance. In addition to the frequent use of extremely loud sounds which have a high density and fill the space, he often distributes the sound sources or loudspeakers around the spectators so that the music comes to them from various angles and distances. In his presentation at Black Mountain College, the audience sat in the center of the space while some performers stood up among them to read, other readings were done from ladders at either end, Merce Cunningham danced around the outer space, and a film was projected on the ceiling and walls.

This manipulation and creative use of the relationship between the presented performance material and the spectator has been developed extensively in Happenings. Spectators are frequently placed in unconventional seating. arrangements so that a performance element which is close to some is far from others and stimuli reach the observer from many different directions. In some arrangements the spectators are free to move and, in selecting their own vantage points, control the spatial relationship themselves. At other times they are led through or past spatially separated performance units much as medieval audiences passed from one station to another.

A major aspect of directional and environmental manipulations is not merely that different spectators experience stimuli at different intensities but that they may not experience some of the material at all. This is intentional, and unavoidable in a situation that is much like a three-ring circus.

If a circus were a work of art, it would be an excellent

example of a Happening. Except for the clowns (and perhaps the man with the lions who pretends that they are vicious), the performances are non-matrixed. The acrobats, jugglers, and animal trainers are "merely" carrying out their activities. The grips or stagehands become performers, too, as they dismantle and rig the equipment—demonstrating that non-matrixed performing exists at all levels of difficulty. The structure of a three-ring circus makes use of simultaneous as well as sequential compartments. There is no information structure: the acts do not add meaning to one another, and one can be fully "understood" without any of the others. At the same time the circus is a total performance and not just the sum of its parts. The flow of processions alternates with focused activity in the rings. Animal acts or acrobatic acts are presented at the same time. Sometimes all but one of the simultaneous acts end at the same moment, concentrating the spectators' previously scattered attention on a single image. Perhaps tumblers and riders are presented early in the program, and a spatial progression is achieved by ending the program with the high wire and trapeze artists. And the circus, even without its traditional tent, has strong environmental aspects. The exhibits of the side show, the menagerie, and the uniformed vendors in the aisles are all part of the show. Sometimes small flashlights with cords attached are hawked to the children: whenever the lights are dimmed, the whole space is filled with hundreds of tiny lights being swung in circles.

But although the acrobat may be seen as an archetypal example of non-matrixed performing, he can be something else. In Vsevolod Meyerhold's biomechanics, actors were trained as acrobats and gymnasts. The actor functioned as a machine, and the constructivist set was merely an arrangement of platforms, ramps, swings, ladders, and other nonrepresentational elements that the performer could use. But the performers were still matrixed by place and character. Although the set did not indicate a particular place, the dialogue and situations made it clear. Biomechanics was used merely as a way of projecting the characters of the story. An actor turned a somersault to express rage or performed a salto-mortale to show exaltation. Calm and unrest could both be signified on the high wire rather than in the usual ways. Determination could be projected from a trapeze. Although biomechanics used movements which, out of context, were non-matrixed acrobatics, it used them within place and character matrices created by an information structure.

The non-matrixed performing in Happenings is of several types. Occasionally people are used somewhat as inanimate objects. In *Washes* by Claes Oldenburg, for example, a motionless girl covered with balloons floated on her back in the swimming pool where the piece was being presented while a man bit the balloons and exploded them. At other times the simple operation of theatrical machinery becomes part of the performance: in *Washes* a record player and a motion picture projector were turned on and off in plain view of the audience; the "lifeguard" merely walked around the pool and helped with certain props. Most non-matrixed performing is more complicated, however. It might be thought of as combining the image quality of the first type with the purposeful functioning of the second. At one point in *Washes*, for example, four men dove into the pool and pushed sections of silver flue pipe back and forth along a red clothes line. There was no practical purpose in shoving and twisting the pipes, but it was real activity. Manufactured character or situation had nothing to do with it. The men did not pretend to be anyone other than themselves, nor did they pretend—unlike the swimmers in *Dead End* or *Wish You Were Here*—that the water they were in was anything other than what it actually was: in this case a health club pool with spectators standing around the edge.

When acting is called for in a Happening, it almost always exists in a rudimentary form. Because of the absence of an information structure, the job of acting tends to fall into its basic elements. Perhaps an emotion is created and projected as it was by the exaggerated frenzy with which the man in *Washes* bit the balloons attached to the floating girl. Although the rate or tempo of this action had no necessary connection with character, and the activity could have been carried out in a non-matrixed manner, it could not be denied that the agitated and mock-ferocious quality that was dominant was acting. The acted qualities stood out and remained isolated because they did not fit into a character matrix or into a larger situation. Other facets of acting—"playing an attitude," place, details of characterization, etc.—are also found in Happenings, but they are usually isolated and function as a very weak matrix.

This is not to say that emotion of any sort during a performance is necessarily acted. Although much non-matrixed performance is comparatively expressionless, it would be erroneous to think that this type of performing is without emotion. Certainly feelings are expressed in the "non-matrixed performing" of everyday life: in the runner's face as he breaks the tape, in the professor's intonation and stress during his lecture, in the owner's attitude as he handles his dog in a dog show. The important point is that emotions apparent during a non-matrixed performance are those of the performer himself. They are not intentionally created, and they are not the natural result of the individual's attitude toward the piece, of the particular task being performed, or of the particular situation of being in front of an audience. Without acted emotions to mask his own feelings, the performer's own attitudes are more apt to become manifest than they are in traditional theatre.

Of course acting and non-matrixed performing have certain elements in common. When the production of various kinds of information is eliminated from the actor's task, certain requirements still remain. They are the same requirements that exist for performers of any kind. Concentration, for example, is as important to athletes and Happeners as it is to actors, and stage presence—the degree to which a person can mask or control feelings of nervousness, shyness, uncertainty, etc.—is equally useful to actors, public speakers, and musicians.[3]

One final point about performance in the new theatre con-

[3] The *use* of stage presence is an aesthetic question. Some performances place a high degree of emphasis upon it, while in others it is intentionally excluded or performers are employed *because* they are somewhat ill at ease.

cerns the question of improvisation and indeterminacy. Indeterminacy means that limits within which the performers are free to make choices are provided by the creator of the piece: a range of alternatives is made available from which the performer may select. Thus in a musical composition the number of notes to be played within a given time period may be given but not the notes themselves; the pitch ranges may be indicated for given durations but not the specific notes required. Indeterminacy is used in the new theatre when, for example, the number of steps a performer should take is limited but the direction is optional; when the type of action is designated but no specific action is given; etc. The choices involved in indeterminacy may be made before the actual performance, but they are most frequently left until the moment of presentation in an attempt to insure spontaneity.

Indeterminacy is not the same as improvisation. Although spontaneity may be a goal of both, it is also the goal of much precisely detailed acting. The primary difference between indeterminacy and improvisation is the amount of momentary, on the spot creativity which is involved. Not only is the detail—the apt comment, the *bon mot,* the unexpected or unusual reaction—central to improvisation, but the form and structure of a scene may also be changed. Even when, as was common in *Commedia dell'Arte,* the general outline of the scene is set, the performer is responding to unfamiliar material and providing in return his inventions, which require a response. As evidenced by the so-called improvisational theatres such as Second City, an improvisation loses these values once it has been repeated a few times. It no longer is an improvisation, and most of these groups make no pretense among themselves that it is. In indeterminacy the alternatives are quite clear, although the exact choice may not be made until performance. And the alternatives *do not matter:* one is as good as another. Since the performers usually function independently and do not respond to the choices made by the other performers, no give-and-take is involved. The situation is not "open-ended" as it is in improvisation.

Thus the four men who manipulated the sections of pipe in

Washes, for example, did no creative work although the details of their actions and procedure were different during each performance. They merely embodied the image of man-and-pipe which Oldenburg had created. They were not, in the true sense, improvising. Only the type of behavior mattered and not the details. Whether they swam for a while rather than "working," whether they twisted this length of pipe rather than that one, whether they worked together or individually, did not matter provided they kept within the directed limits. The image was the same each night.

A somewhat related attitude is the acceptance of incidental aspects of audience reaction and environmental occurrences as *part* of the production. One of Cage's most notorious musical compositions is *4' 33"*—four minutes and thirty-three seconds of silence by the musician or musicians performing it. The non-playing (in addition to focusing the "performer" aspects of the piece) allows any "incidental" sounds—perhaps traffic noises or crickets outside the auditorium, the creak of seats, coughing and whispering in the audience—to become "music." This exploitation and integration of happenstance occurrences unique to each performance into the performance itself is another common, but not universal, trait of the new theatre.

One method of assuring completely alogical structure in a work is to use chance methods. Beginning in about 1951 Cage used chance operations such as a system of coin tossing derived from *I Ching*, the Chinese *Book of Changes*. In a method close to pure chance, he determined the placement of notes in certain compositions by marking the imperfections in the score paper. In the Happening which he presented during the summer of 1952 at Black Mountain College the point of entry and the duration of the various performance elements were fixed by chance techniques. Cage's *Theatre Piece* of 1960 can be performed by one to eight musicians, singers, actors, dancers, and is unusual in that it provides an elaborate *method* (including the use of plastic overlays) of determining individual "scores," but it does not designate the actions, sounds, phrases, etc.—several groups of which are selected to be the raw material for the chance operations.

The use of chance and indeterminacy in composition are aspects of a wide concern with methods and procedure in the new theatre. Another approach to the question of method is illustrated by a *Graphis* by Dick Higgins (who also studied with Cage) in which a linear pattern is marked out on the floor of the performance space with words written at various points. Performers may move only along the lines, and they perform preselected actions corresponding to each word when they arrive at that word. Thus the repeated actions and limited lines of movement create visual and rhythmic patterns which freely structure the work in an alogical way.

Jackson MacLow, another of Cage's students, applied chance methods to the materials of the traditional drama. For *The Marrying Maiden,* for example, he selected characters and speeches from the *I Ching.* The order and duration of speeches and the directions for rate, volume, inflection, and manner of speaking were all independently ascribed to the material by chance techniques. Five different tempos ranging from "Very Slow" to "Very Fast" and five different amplitudes ranging from "Very Soft" to "Very Loud" were used. The attitudes to be acted were selected and placed into the script by the application of random number methods to a list of 500 adverbs or adverbial phrases ("smugly," "religiously," "apingly," etc.) compiled by MacLow. Although the delivery of the lines in *The Marrying Maiden* is more closely controlled than in a traditional script, no movements, business, or actions are given. Staging is left to the director or actors. When the play was presented by The Living Theatre in 1960 and 1961, the physical activity worked out by Judith Malina, the director, was fixed. Other actions were inserted at random intervals by the use of an "action pack" of about 1,200 cards containing stage directions ("scratch yourself," "kiss the nearest woman," "use any three objects in an action,") which were given to the performers by a visible stage manager who rolled dice to determine his own behavior.

In many of the works by Dick Higgins the operations of chance shift emphatically onto the performance. In *The Tart*, for example, selection by chance or taste is made from among the given characters, speeches, and cues by the performer or director, who then decides on actions to supplement the chosen material. Since at least some of the behavior or effects which cue the speeches and actions are provided by one or more "special performers," a complicated cueing situation exists, creating a performance *pattern* which is different each time, although the performance *materials* remain constant.

Since the chance performances of MacLow and Higgins make basic use of acting, the fundamental material of traditional theatre, there is some justification for retaining them in the "play" or "drama" category. They can be called *chance plays* or *alogical drama*. They are not Happenings. As with other definitions in the new theatre, however, these terms can only be applied by measuring central tendency. Plays obviously use materials other than acting; Happenings may use acting as part of the performance. It then becomes a question of whether acting is the *primary* element, as in a play, or whether the emphasis is on non-matrixed performing, physical effect, or a balance between several components, as in a Happening.

The recent production of *The Tart* is an example of the difficulty that can result when one tries to categorize a particular performance without making up pointless terms. Reading the script, there seems to be no question that the basic performance element is supposed to be acting and that it is a chance play. In the actual production at the Sunnyside Garden boxing arena in Queens, however, acting was used much less than it could have been, and physical effects were added. Because of this, the emphasis was shifted past the borderline between Happenings and chance theatre. This, in itself, is not important, but the way in which it came about makes clearer how to apply the terms I have been using.

In order to understand the apparent shift away from acting in the performance of *The Tart*, two things must be remembered. In the first place, distinctions between matrixed and non-matrixed performing are not made on the basis of acting style or on the basis of good or bad acting. Both naturalistic acting, in which the performer disappears within the character, and formalized acting, which makes use of "artificial" gesture and speech, develop equally strong matrices. The acrobatic performers in *Le Cocu magnifique* were acting. And the poor actor—unless he gives up completely and drops out of character to ask for a line—is, like the good actor, providing a supply of character-place data. The work may be more obvious in one case and the matrices demonstrated or indicated rather than implied, but this is basically an aesthetic question rather than a formal one.

In the second place, neither costumes nor dialogue have any necessary relationship to acting. A costume or a line of dialogue is—like a prop, a particular kind of light, or the setting—merely another piece of information. It may be related to character material which is acted or to other information and thus help to form a strong matrix, but a non-matrixed performer may also wear a costume or speak.

The Tart makes great demands upon actors. The performers do not speak to each other and "play scenes" in the way possible, for example, with the alogical verbal material of Jackson MacLow's *Verdurous Sanguinaria*. The dialogue of *The Tart* usually consists of speeches attributed to some other character, and something of that character is supposed to be superimposed upon the base character when the line is given. Obviously, in order to keep "in character," highly skilled actors are needed, and when the performers cannot sustain the base character, as happened in this case, acting disintegrates into disparate lines and actions. Although the performers are required to select their own actions, which can strengthen the character matrix and ease the complicated and difficult task, many of them in this production chose to use arbitrary or meaningless movement, which only destroyed any character matrix they might have established. One or two of the performers, experienced in Happenings, made no attempt to act. Thus the final effect was one in which acting was subordinate to effect and to non-matrixed performing. In performance *The Tart* turned from a chance play into a Happening.

Just as the words "play" and "drama" have a historical usage which should not be replaced with "Happening" or "Event" unless the fundamental elements are different, the word "dance" has an accepted meaning which takes precedence over any new terminology. And certain contemporary developments in dance are a very important part of the new theatre. Although these developments are the result of progressive aesthetic changes within the field, the form has been brought to that point where many formal and stylistic similarities exist between contemporary dance works and pieces presented by non-dancers which are not referred to as "dance." Significant creative exchange has become possible between disciplines that have been thought of as isolated. One pronounced and important characteristic of the new theatre is the tendency to reduce or eliminate the traditionally strong divisions of drama, dance, opera, etc.

The changes in dance which give it a place in the new theatre parallel those which are exemplified by Events, Happenings, and chance theatre, but did not necessarily derive from them. For example, Merce Cunningham created *16 Dances* by chance method in 1951—the year before Cage's presentation at Black Mountain College. The order of passages and even the order of movements within one passage were determined by tossing coins. (Cage, who has worked closely with Cunningham for many years and was working with chance techniques at that time, composed the music for the piece by setting a fixed procedure for moving on a chart containing the noises, tones, and aggregates of sound that would be used in the composition.) Since Cunningham's early work, much investigation into chance, game, and indeterminacy methods and various other alogical structures has been undertaken by dancers, especially by Ann Halprin's Dancers' Workshop and by Robert Dunn, whose classes at Cunningham's studio in 1960–62 eventually developed into the Judson Dance Theatre.

As structure in dance became alogical and made use of simultaneous performances that were not interrelated (except that they were concurrently presented to the spectator), the manner of performance has also changed. Of course certain types of dancing have always been non-matrixed. No character or place is created and projected in ballroom dancing (which, it might be pointed out, almost always has an audience, although that is not its orientation), and acrobatic dancing, tap dancing, soft shoe dancing, and the like are all non-matrixed—unless, of course, they appear as part of the action in a play. But, from the stories of ballet to the psychological projections of Modern Dance, the dance as an art form has generally made use of character and place matrices. In recent years, however, story, plot, character, situation, "ecstasy," personal expression, and self-dramatization have all dropped away, and dance has made use of non-matrixed performing.

The separation of dance from music is perhaps one of the factors responsible for the shift. Musical accompaniment functions in part as an emotional matrix which "explains" dancers. Think, for example, of how much expression and character can be given to the film image of a blank face or even the back of a head by the music on the sound track. In John Cage's scores for many of Merce Cunningham's dances, music and movement merely fill the same time period without relationship. Some of Mary Wigman's dances just after World War I and almost all of the dances in the new theatre entirely eliminated music; thus "interpretation" is no longer a factor, and the possibility of non-matrixed performing is increased.

As character, emotional continuity, and a sense of created locale have been eliminated from dance, walking, running, falling, doing calisthenics, and other simple activities from everyday life have become dance elements. No attempt is made to embellish these actions, and it does not take years of training to "dance" them. Merce Cunningham did a piece called *Collage* at Brandeis University in 1953 in which he used fifteen untrained "dancers" who performed simple, ordinary movements and activities such as running and hair combing. A number of "non-dancers" are performing members of the Judson Dance Theatre [4] in New York City.

The concern for activity with its concomitant movement rather than for movement in itself—for *what* is done rather than *how* it is done—brings much new dance very close to Happenings and Events. And just as any performance may be called "music" with the justification that sound is involved, almost any performance may be referred to as "dance" when human movement is involved. Works which are not formally distinguishable from Happenings have been called dance pieces. Actually the most important differences among many of the performances in the new theatre—whether done by painters, sculptors, musicians, dancers, or professional theatre people— exist on stylistic rather than formal grounds. One wonders what difference it would make if *Check* by Robert Morris, for example, were called a Happening, and Claes Oldenburg's *Washes* were referred to as a dance.

Certain works have come out of the new theatre and out of the creative climate fostered by Cage which have pushed "performance" beyond the limits of theatre and which offer new insights into the nature of performing and of theatre. Cage advocated the elimination of boundaries between art and life. The acceptance of chance is an acceptance of the laws of nature; and life, as illustrated in 4' 33", always particpates in the totality of the perceived work of art. (This way of thinking means, for example, that a painting or sculpture is not the same in the gallery as it is in the studio.)

Performance and audience are both necessary to have theatre. But it might be thought that it is this very separation of

[4] Although traditional dance movements and techniques are not excluded, this emphasis on relatively simple kinds of movement has led to the style being labeled "anti-dance." In lieu of a more accurate term, the name has some usefulness, but the intent of the dancers is not to oppose or destroy dance but to eliminate what seem to be unnecessary conventions and restrictions, to approach movement in a fresh way, and to open new formal areas.

spectator and work which is responsible for an "artificiality" of the form, and many Happenings and related pieces have attempted to "break down" the "barrier" between presentation and spectator and to make the passive viewer a more active participator. At any rate, works have recently been conceived which, since they are to be performed without an audience—a totally original and unprecedented development in art—might be called Activities.

In some of George Brecht's pieces the question of an audience seems ambiguous. Brecht's work implies that any performance piece has an aesthetic value for its performer or creator which is distinct from its value for an audience: the performance of *any* piece without an audience is a certain kind of art. Some of his things, such as the untitled child-thermometer-clock piece, are so intimate that spectators are obviously not intended or required.

Activities make it possible to work with time and space dimensions that would be very difficult or impossible in theatre. In *Chair* by Robert Ashley, for example, a wooden chair is variously transformed on each of six successive days. The lines in Stanley Brouwn's *Phonedrawings* exist only in the mind of the performer, who is aware that if the locations he has called on the telephone were connected (in the same way the child connects numbered dots to make a picture appear) the image he has chosen would actually exist on a vast scale. These works emphasize the private, proprioceptive, and cerebral aspects of Activities.

Allan Kaprow has performed pieces which also eliminate the audience but function on a much larger scale. Some of them, using many performers, resembled his Happenings except for the absence of spectators. The more recent pieces, although involving sizable numbers of performers, are more widely distributed through space and time so that the participants are frequently entirely separated from each other. Ken Dewey's recent works have mixed both Activity sections and units in which the assembled people functioned in the traditional passive manner of spectators.

Although these works, like Kaprow's *Eat* Environment, are outside the limits of theatre, they are related to the performance mentality, and they help to clarify some of the attitudes and concepts of the new theatre as well as providing fresh theoretical positions from which to evaluate theatre as a whole.

John Cage is emphasized as the touchstone of the new theatre for at least two reasons. In the first place, the body of his work —writings and lectures as well as musical compositions and performance pieces—gives clear precedents for many later developments. Secondly, many of the younger artists in the new theatre actually studied with Cage, although each creates in his own manner.

But there are at least as many reasons why the formulation I have presented is not wholly true or valid. As a simplification, it glosses over the exceptions and degrees of shading that any complete account should have. Actually, the new theatre has been in existence long enough for widening aesthetic ripples to spread far from the source. Each artist changes it. It has moved in various directions, making use of established techniques as well as the most recent developments in other fields and disciplines. Many of the artists producing Happenings, for example, are not fundamentally in sympathy with Cage's views, and their work is stylistically very different.

The emphasis on Cage may have implied that he is a completely original artist. This of course is not true. Completely original artists—like Dylan Thomas' "eggs laid by tigers"—do not exist. Actually each of the dimensions of Cage's work was prefigured in the work of the Futurists and the Dadaists, in Marinetti, Duchamp, and others. (Of course, much of this material had been available to everyone for a good number of years. It is to Cage's credit that he saw what was in it while others apparently did not.)

A sketch of the earlier history and origins of the new theatre would have to begin at least with the Italian Futurists, whose *"bruitisme,"* the use of everyday sounds and noises rather than those produced by traditional musical instruments, can be traced through Dada, the compositions of Erik Satie and Edgar Varése, and, finally, electronic music, which has as its material a sound spectrum of unprecedented width and variety. Although the Futurists apparently did not add non-musical elements to their performances, their theoretical position provided the basis for the later expansion of music into performance.

In addition to their own "noise music" performed by "instruments" such as baby rattles and jangled keys and tin cans, the Dadaists in Zürich during World War I and later in Paris read and recited simultaneous poems and manifestos which were an early form of compartmentalization. (These and the Dada distortion of the lecture into a work of art prefigure certain aspects of Cage's lectures.) Unrelated "acts" were often performed at the same time, and the Dadaists presented what would now be referred to as Events: Philippe Soupault in his *Le célèbre illusioniste* (*The Famous Magician*) released balloons of various colors each bearing the name of a famous man; Walter Serner, instead of reading a poem, placed a bouquet of flowers at the feet of a dressmaker's dummy; in their *Noir Cacadou* Richard Huelsenbeck and Tristan Tzara waddled around in a sack with their heads in a piece of pipe; Jean Arp recited his poems from inside a huge hat, and Georges Ribemont-Dessaignes danced inside a giant funnel. The Dadaists even staged a mock trial in front of an audience with "witnesses" called for the prosecution and the defense.

The intentional use of chance so important to Cage and some of the new theatre was also used by the Dadaists. Tristan Tzara composed and recited poems by mixing cards with words on them in a hat and drawing out the cards one at a time. Arp and Duchamp used chance in making paintings and constructions.

Surrealism also had its impact on the new theatre. It proposed the irrational as the material of art and stressed the dream, the obsessive act, the psychic accident; it supported automatism and chance as creative techniques and thus—after being driven from Europe to this country by World War II— provided the basis for Abstract Expressionism. (Although Cage accepted this concern with method, he differed sharply from later creators of Happenings such as Oldenburg and Whitman who stressed the unconscious affective aspects in their work.)

The Abstract Expressionist mentality which pervaded the New York art world in the late 1950's was one of the contributing factors in bringing painters into the performing arts. The *act* of painting rather than the completed composition had become the creative focus. At the same time painting and sculpture had a long tradition, in which Dada and Surrealism played their parts, of assemblage—the fabricating of a work from disparate objects and materials. Thus the artists found nothing strange about assembling a theatrical work from various types of alogically related performance material.

The new theatre is not important merely because it is new. But if it is agreed that a work of art may be important only if it is new—an aesthetic position which cannot be elaborated or defended here—then these works deserve serious consideration. Not only should they suggest to any practicing theatre artist new directions in which his work may go, but they represent several of the most significant developments in the history of theatre art.

In this theatre "suspension of disbelief" is not operative, and the absence of character and situation precludes identification. Thus the traditional mode of experiencing theatre, which has dominated both players and spectators for thousands of years, is altered.

As I have tried to show, structure and, almost always, the manner of performing are radically different in the new theatre. These innovations place theatre—in a very limited way —in some equivalency with the other arts. If painting and sculpture, for example, have not yet exhausted the possibilities of their nonobjective breakthrough (which occurred only a few years after the start of this century), and if music has not yet begun to assimilate all the implications of its new-found electronic materials, there is every reason to feel that there will also be a fruitful aesthetic future for the new theatre.

ORIGINALE, I

In September, 1964, *Originale* by the German composer Karl-heinz Stockhausen was presented at Judson Hall as part of the Second Annual New York Festival of the Avant-Garde. Judson Hall—not to be confused with Judson Memorial Church in Greenwich Village, which has long been a center for avant-garde performances—is located directly opposite Carnegie Hall on the north side of Fifty-seventh Street near Seventh Avenue. You walk up stairs to reach the hall itself, a large rectangular room with a flat floor, mirrors on the side walls, a small balcony at one end, and a proscenium stage at the other. Most frequently, it is rented for music recitals.

For *Originale* the hall was transformed. A tall complicated metal scaffolding stood against one of the side walls. Folding chairs for the spectators filled the stage and almost all of the space in the main section of the hall where they were arranged in groups facing in different directions with only fairly narrow aisles between. Tape recorders and sound equipment, spotlights, a piano, an intercom for the lights, racks of clothes, a motion picture screen, closed circuit television with camera and receiving set, and elaborate groupings of drums, gongs, and other percussion equipment were scattered about. At each of the five performances there was "standing room only" attendance, the somewhat bewildered, bemused, and nervous spectators generating the kind of feeling one sometimes gets at an important sporting event.

Originale lasted for exactly ninety-four minutes. Stockhausen's music, both on tape and produced "live," was the most pervasive and important element in the piece. The script indicated what type of activity should be going on at each particular moment, and the performers were guided by a centrally placed clock. For example, at the twenty-eighth minute

Actor V began a "monologue from religious drama." The particular choice of monologue and drama were left up to the actor, but certain characteristics of the reading, which lasted until the forty-first minute, were determined by the script: i.e., "Humorous (40″) with 2 brief tragic moments."

Allan Kaprow was the "director," and he actually assembled the "cast" and conducted rehearsals as well as taking part in the presentation. Max Neuhaus and James Tenney performed the music theatrically at percussion and piano. Robert Breer ran the closed circuit television, screening views of the audience and the performance; late in the piece, one of his films was also projected. Allan Ginsberg read poetry at the first performance and intoned a prayer to Krishna at the others. Marjorie Strider was the "hat check girl," bringing various clothes to Max and Jim and helping them to change. Jackson MacLow, who read in Greek at one point, and Dick Higgins were among the five "actors." Lette Eisenhauer and Olga Kluver were "models"; their undressing and posing received very favorable notice in the New York newspapers, which gave the production wider coverage than any other similar piece has yet received. Dressed in old clothes, I entered at the thirty-fifth minute, sold current evening newspapers to the spectators or cast for exactly two minutes, and exited again.

At the next to last performance, the chimpanzee was caught, as I recall, in a traffic jam in New Jersey and could not get to the hall. The large dogs were also absent for some reason. Charlotte Moorman, who was coproducing the festival, was frantic. The script called for animals, and we had to have at least one. The performance had already begun when she asked the girl who had previously been walking the dogs to find a replacement. The girl rushed down to Fifty-seventh Street and asked for help from the first person she met who was walking a dog. It was an elderly woman dressed in black; the dog was smallish with a lot of curly white hair. The woman agreed.

As it was described to me later, the woman entered the hall and looked around. She did not really know why a dog was needed or what was taking place. The packed, cluttered space reverberated with Stockhausen's concrete music. The lights changed constantly, reflected in the mirrored walls. Performers climbed on the scaffolding and moved here and there through the spectators who faced each other in unusual groupings, crowded the stage and filled the balcony. Perhaps the television was on, actors were yelling through bullhorns or whispering readings, people were undressing, or someone was feeding the fish who swam in small hanging bowls. "Ah," said the elderly woman with understanding, "Futurism!"

After the performance, I was to talk with the woman and learn that she had been singing leading roles in the opera in Milan, I believe it was, when the Futurists were giving concerts there. She would not say whether it was before World War I or immediately afterward. Her sister still lived in Italy and had a lot of material on the Futurists; I was very excited, but the woman never called me to say that she had received documents and would translate them.

As it was, I stood at the back of the crowded stage knowing nothing of the procurement of the replacement animal and watched the erect woman in black walk carefully and simply through the turbulence with her dog. The dog was quite nondescript. His short legs, stocky body, and floppy-eared head were completely hidden in shaggy white hair. But there was something fascinating about him. I watched him intently, thinking that the unusual quality of the moment must be due to its comparison with the preceding evenings, and that it would be unavailable to the spectators who were seeing the piece for the first time. I knew the woman and her dog did not really belong. Their age—the dog, too, seemed old—and dignity were accentuated by the performance of which they had become a part, I thought. But ultimately, I could not understand the peculiar power of their presence. Later I learned that the dog was blind. He had been attacked by a big dog in Central Park. Before she would lead him out among the spectators, the woman had asked that water on the floor from preceding activities be taken up. Being blind, the dog would not walk into water. And his movements, of course, were not quite like those of a normal dog, although I had not understood their meaning as, with sightless eyes covered by his curly hair, he helped us with our performance.

Chance methodology might say that at a given moment any one of a given number of alternatives is as good as any other: One dog is as good as another in *Originale*. But I am often shocked at the unique and unpredictable qualities generated by accidents and an *un*methodical use of chance, as this was. At any rate, the woman and her dog also seemed pleased. They came back to participate again the following evening.

Objective
Dance

On Friday and Saturday November 17 and 18, 1967, a dance choreographed by Deborah Hay and titled *Group One* was presented at The School of Visual Arts in New York. *Group One* can be seen to exemplify a general "movement" in dance, now still in its formative stages, whose radical innovation is, I believe, as significant, in aesthetic terms, as was the development of Modern Dance in the early part of this century. The purpose of this essay is to analyze the characteristics of this new kind of dance as typified by *Group One*, to clarify the differences between it and more traditional forms of dance, and thereby to suggest the importance of this kind of work.

In using only a single example to represent what has already been referred to as a "movement," there is the possibility of exaggerating the uniqueness or historical position of the particular piece and seeming to slight other dancer-choreographers who have been working along similar lines. A detailed and accurate history of the new dance form is not the issue at the moment, however, and a single example is sufficient to illustrate the theoretical points involved. Deborah Hay's piece, although relatively short, is an excellent "pure" study of elements which occur with varying consistency and clarity in other works. (It is also a work, in my opinion, of great aesthetic interest and impact, but value judgments of artistic worth are also not our concern here.)

The movement, which has been somewhat vaguely referred to as "avant-garde dance" and many of whose members first worked publicly with the Judson Dance Theatre in the early 1960's, shows as much superficial diversity of style as any other major aesthetic grouping. The consideration of all the variations, techniques, and experiments—many of which touched or passed beyond the limits of dance itself—presented by the "members" of the movement would cloud, rather than clarify, what I see as the basic issues which were crystallized in *Group One*. The movement has also been referred to as "anti-dance," a name that is both quite apt and very inappropriate. It is fitting in that much of the new work comes about, or can be seen, as a reaction against traditional forms of dance. But it is only these forms of dance to which the artists seem to be opposed and not dance itself. The dancers and choreographers feel they are doing dance and some of them resent the label "anti-dance" because it may be interpreted as "non-dance" or the rejection of all dance dimensions.

Deborah Hay's *Group One* began with a black-and-white motion picture. In every shot, although there was some camera movement and the scale and angle of the pictures changed somewhat, the camera was always aimed toward the corner of a room where white walls converged at the center of the frame. There were five basic sequences in the film, intercut or "punctuated" by static shots of the corner and by black: (1) one at a time, following no discernible system, twenty-two people in dark suits and dresses walked from behind the camera into the corner, filling it with a closely spaced human wedge; the men and women were facing somewhat toward the camera, parallel to the right wall, and after a moment the whole group walked forward along the wall as a unit, using short, quick steps which allowed smooth, almost uninflected transport; the group kept in the wedge until they disappeared from view and only the empty corner could be seen; (2) the men and women walked quickly into their positions in the corner at the same time, the momentary confusion changing into the motionless human wedge filling the space; after a moment, the wedge again moved as a unit along the right wall and out of the motion picture frame, leaving the corner empty; (3) a line of performers walked into the corner to stand along the right wall, and other lines of decreasing length followed until the triangular group was again formed, this time facing to the left; using the same short, sliding steps, the people moved as a wedge along the left wall and out of the frame; (4) a number of people moved into the corner and stood facing out toward the camera; only half of the wedge had been formed, and after a moment the remaining performers took their places but remained facing into the corner toward the first group; they turned simultaneously, completing the wedge, which moved directly toward the camera and past it, leaving the corner empty; (5) the corner was again filled as the men and women moved into place at the same time and stood motionless facing the camera; a single man walked to the group, slipped into his place at the rear apex of the triangle, and the completed unit stood motionless. The film closed with brief shots of the motionless triangular mass of people facing parallel first to the right and then to the left wall.

As soon as the film ended, lights came on illuminating the performance area. They were to remain on without change until the end of the piece. At the same time a tape recording started which was to play steadily without any "build" or development until the dance was almost over. The tape seemed to contain the voices of several men and women making soft moaning, fricative, and animal noises. The tempo was slow and steady; at times amid the windlike whispers and soft cackling and mooing, crooned half-intelligible words could be heard.

Five men and three women wearing black semiformal attire stood with twelve-foot wooden poles painted white. At unequal and unpredictable intervals during the performance the eight performers, taking their cue from an unseen "conductor," would simultaneously lower the poles forward from their vertical positions, bring them together so that there was a brief "sound cluster" of wood striking wood, and rotate them back to the vertical.

While the tape recording played and the bursts of activity with the wooden poles continued independently, two men and three women, also dressed in black suits and dresses, performed the central movement element of the piece. Twice they entered through two doors that backed the performance space, stood motionless for a few seconds, and exited again. (The cues for all entrances were taken from offstage stop watches.) Walking into the performance area simultaneously, they briefly stood in a line facing away from the audience, then dispersed to walk out the doors or up the aisles. Several times, lines formed and broke up. The five performers assembled (in random order that tended to change with each performance) in a line facing the audience with their arms around each other's waists: slowly and evenly they changed their weight from one foot to the other, rocking to one side and then to the other as a unit. They joined hands and went through a sequence of simple, simultaneous, repetitive stepping forward and stamping. A circle formed three times and was immediately broken. The five kneeled in a line facing away from the spectators for several beats. They walked into a line facing the audience again and performed a sequence of stepping forward in unison and reaching up, snapping the palms of their hands outward at the top of the move. Still in line, abreast, they performed a sequence of rocking and simultaneous knee bends to either side. The steadily rocking line began to disperse, the people at the ends detaching themselves and walking away. Finally, only the center person stood alone, still rocking. The "music" on the tape had stopped, and the lone performer rocked in silence except when the long wooden poles were occasionally lowered, seemed to tangle together in visual and auditory confusion for a moment, and then returned to white, motionless, verticals. From the scattered places to which they had disappeared, the four performers walked back to rejoin the fifth and again form a line. The line shifted to arrange itself for the first time at an oblique angle to the audience, the performers' backs somewhat turned to the spectators. They stood motionless for a moment. The lights went out, and the performance was over: it had lasted seventeen minutes, including the initial six minutes of film.

The performance on film in *Group One* is one example of a particular use of human movement and space, the traditional materials of the dance, in a new way. (From the point of view of understanding the general theoretical points involved, it does not matter whether the images were on film or were carried out in the presentation by live performers: it was the film of a dance.) The performers were not used for their physical characteristics, and no ability or special technique was required to perform the movements. The people, either walking singly or moving in lines, were merely used as elements out of which an architectonic or sculptural human mass could be assembled in relationship to an actual architectural element, the corner of the room. Various ways of assembling the triangular mass, the possibilities of orientation in relationship to the walls making the corner, and the various basic directional possibilities available to the moving mass were the elements out of which the time structure of the dance was composed.

In contrast, the basic movement section actually performed by the live dancers made no use of masses or closed architectonic shapes (except for the circle which was merely suggested before it disappeared). Density, flow, and spatial extension were qualified by the performers who came together, formed linear figures, and dispersed. The rate or tempo of movement was constant and unaltered, having no climaxes and few passages of stasis. Progression, development, and "build" existed entirely in supraindividual terms and not in the performance of any single dancer. The line that periodically assembled and disintegrated existed at times only in simple relationship to the particular volumetric space of the performance area and, directionally, to the audience; at other times, like the traditional chorus with its simultaneous synchronized movements, it took on particular qualities or characteristics unrelated to the personal styles of the individual dancers who composed the moving unit.

The structure of the long main section of *Group One* was based upon two elements, the "voice music" of the tape and the visual-aural image with the poles, that did not develop, and one element, the dancers, that presented a developing series of movement images. In its placement, for example, of the "pole people" in a right-angle line on a raised level at one side of the main performance space, the performance made use of specific physical aspects of the particular place of performance. But the structure, style, imagery, etc. of *Group One* are not the issue here. The performance is merely intended as an example of a new kind of dance, and it is the characteristics of this new form and its relationship to dance in general to which we must direct our attention.

One of the key issues of the new dance lies in the use of "non-dancers" and the concomitant elimination of specialized dance technique. Probably all of the performers in *Group One* had danced socially, as most of us do, and had perhaps studied ballet or Modern Dance as many young people do, but they had none of the habits of movement or posture that are the natural and, to some extent, unconscious by-product of years of training and performance in any style of dance. Just as, independent of actual success or failure, the experience of a first baseman in baseball, for example, is communicated by his movements as he handles the special glove and "covers" the base, we recognize a "dancer," quite independently from value judgments of good or bad, by his performance poise and habits. In other words, although dance technique is related to the exigencies of particular styles, there seem to be basic characteristics or "common denominators" of behavior that separate what we call dance from the movement of everyday life. The technique of all dance as we traditionally know it is based on two interrelated factors (1) a complete muscular attentiveness, and (2) a smooth energy flow. Because of the complex physical demands of traditional dance and the emphasis on the visual unity or wholeness of any movement or position, the dancer's entire body must be in a state of muscular alertness. Even the muscles which are not moving contribute to the dance, and a dancer "dances" even when he is motionless. Smooth energy flow has been required by common stylistic values of beauty and grace and by the relationship of movement to rhythms which are frequently subtle and demanding. Harsh, awkward, or rough movements are indicated by stylistic conventions and their contrast with other movements rather than actually being carried out on a muscular level. The movements of everyday life are "smoothed out" in a variety of ways when they are mirrored in dance. These two factors of complete muscular attentiveness and smooth energy flow, together with their relationship to conventional dance styles and learned performance habits, we may label "danciness." The new dance is based in part on a reaction against this "danciness" and attempts to reject it.

Webster's dictionary defines "technique" as "The methods or the details of procedure essential to expertness in an art . . ." and the concept of *expertness* is another target of the new dance. Obviously, in works such as *Group One* standards of good-adequate-poor still exist. The pieces are carefully rehearsed for what are sometimes long periods of time. Individual performers improve. One performer may be better than another. Mistakes can be made. But since the movements and timing are simple enough to be performed well by most people without requiring special training or "talent," an outstanding individual performance is impossible. The *tour de force* which is an aesthetic cornerstone of most traditional dance is eliminated when special technique is not necessary. The new dance is not concerned with the perfectability of movement or with the idealization of form. This sets it apart from even such contemporary dance groups as Merce Cunningham's, about which Allen Hughes was able to write in the *New York Times*, "each of their movements becomes an object of near perfect beauty in itself."

One very significant result of the use of simplified movements and the elimination of dance technique is the *objectification* of dance. Dance in the larger sense with its foundations in ritual and social dancing is basically meant to be *done* rather than be seen: it is subjective. The primary experience of dance in general, as distinct from its particular aesthetic uses, lies in performance rather than in observation of a performance. From this point of view, all traditional dance can be seen to depend essentially upon proprioception and kinesthesia—the inner feeling of one's own body in movement—and on the possible relationship of these feelings of self to external spatial information and sound. In traditional performance the connection between dancer and observer is then basically one of empathy. The spectator "reads himself into" the dancer. This process does not have to be as obvious as the track fan tensing as the pole vaulter attempts to clear the bar or the golfer using sympathetic magic as he gives "body English" to his rolling putt. Empathy theory hypothesizes an outwardly passive but inwardly active correspondence between the state of the spectator and the physical movements of the dancer he is watching. In the new dance the subjective empathetic relationship which exists in all traditional performance dance is replaced by an objective relationship in which the observer sees but does not "participate in" the work. Since this objectification is the essential characteristic of the new dance and the one which differentiates it most clearly and importantly from traditional dance, the new form can be called *Objective Dance*.

Objectification is achieved in several ways. Since the body movements are simple and of little kinesthetic interest to the performer himself, there is no impulse to "read oneself into" the dancer. If the observer himself can do the movements, the "fantasy" and "wish fulfillment" aspects of empathy are blocked. Although empathy is not necessarily related to meaning, it is one of the means for "expression" for the performer and "understanding" by the spectator, and Objective Dance, unconcerned with the "communication" of meaning and emotion, also refuses to become involved with information, characterization, situation, place, or any other references outside of itself. The performers' own clothing is used rather than costumes which would create an imaginary identity for their wearers. Settings that would refer to some place other than the performance space itself are not employed. Lighting is used for illumination and structure rather than for mood, symbol, or storytelling. The movements are not indicative of emotions or character; there is no muscular strain or tension; the performers are expressionless, their faces neutral. The observer has no emotional or intellectual cues on which to base projection, reference, or interpretation. Objective Dance does not represent or "mean" anything other than what it is. It is concrete.

Since the movements of Objective Dance do not have the complete muscular attentiveness and smooth energy flow that we recognize as dance, and "danciness" has been replaced by the muscular dynamics of everyday life, can the performers be said to be "dancing"? They can, but only because they are part of the recognizable entity of "a dance." That is, the performance in which they are involved has, as a whole, those qualities of human spatial and movement patterning which we define as "dance." On the individual level, the movements of a single performer may, even though they use only the "technique" of everyday life, repeat, echo, modify themselves, occur rhythmically, and exist in the same kind of formal relationships to which the word "dance" has always been applied. The possibilities of patterning similarities, variations, and differences in movement still exist even when the type of movement is changed. The structuring of three-dimensional space by means of human movement takes place in the new performances as well as the traditional ones, and the change from subjective to objective viewing attitudes does not alter the basic similarities that make for "dance." Although Objective Dance may paradoxically be called "dance without dancers," it is still dance.

Thus the emphasis in Objective Dance shifts from the performer to the choreographer, from musculature to movement in space. (In *Group One,* for example, the dancers' bodies were concealed in ordinary clothing rather than being revealed by the usual costumes of ballet and Modern Dance.) Since there is no emotional "message" or "meaning" to be conveyed by the performers, there is no longer any question of *interpretation* of the work. "Anyone" can perform the piece, and the interpretive artists of traditional dance are not called for. Just as in painting and sculpture, the aesthetic value of the work depends on only a single creative artist. In this sense, too, of a single "external" controlling artist, the new dance may be considered "objective."

Although Don McDonagh, reviewing *Group One* in the *New York Times,* can pejoratively describe "unmotivated entrances and exits," there should be no need at this point in the history of art, or even in the history of dance, to explain and justify formalism. The entrances and exits, as well as all the other elements of *Group One,* were completely unmotivated in terms of "character" or "situation" because these elements were not employed in the piece, but they were entirely justified and "motivated" by the pure spatial and movement structure. In Objective Dance and related works, an element is its own justification. The fact that pure relationships of sensory and spatial elements may have significance quite apart from literal "meaning" should be beyond dispute.

Objectification and the refusal to be involved with emotional or situational fictions does not mean that Objective Dance is "alienated," impersonal, or mechanical. Martha Graham may be considered "human" because she concerns herself with sentiments and passions. Alwin Nikolais may be seen as "inhuman" because we empathize with his mechanical mutants in their science-fiction worlds. But this is the literary imagination at work. Since the performers in *Group One* neither hid their humanness (as precision dancers could do) nor pretended to be someone they were not, the work could be said to be human in the most simple and direct way. The human element of the imprecision resulting from synchronized movements done without precision technique could be considered one of the basic qualities or "colors" of the work.

Nor should the apparent limiting of means through the rejection of technique be a problem. There are no rules as to "how much" of any factor is needed to make a work of art. If Mondrian can create paintings which rank among the greatest of this century by using, at most, five colors including black and white and only straight lines to limit the color areas, and if many artists such as Malevich, Rodchenko, Rauschenberg, and Reinhardt can do paintings using only one hue, there is no need to equate the "amount of art" with the range of means employed.

In summary, we may say that Objective Dance, as exemplified in a pure state by Deborah Hay's *Group One*, makes a distinct break with the dance of the past. Evidenced in the rejection of technique, convention, idealization, story and anecdote, musical accompaniment, interpretation, emotional expression, and other traditional aspects of dance, it manifests itself in a new psychic relationship between the spectator and the work. It must be experienced with a state of mind that has not previously been called for in dance, making it unrewarding and frustrating to those who must empathize and project themselves into the work. But it is a state of mind that has been necessary for half a century when looking at certain painting and sculpture, explaining why Objective Dance has developed in close contact with the world of painting and sculpture and why it seems to be appreciated primarily by those who are involved with those arts. Whether or not a wider and larger audience ever senses its importance in performance, the steps that it has already made are significant indications of a change in the mind and consciousness of man.

Waiting "offstage" after my two-minute stint of selling news-papers in *Originale,* I always made a point of watching Nam June Paik's solo portion of the performance. His intensity and concentration were harsh and theatrical as he poured shaving cream and rice on his head, slowly unrolled a long scroll in front of his face, jumped into a tub of water, and played the piano. At each of the five performances his "routine" seemed to change somewhat. On the last evening, he had just begun when three well-dressed men stood up from their seats in the audience, walked directly to him, methodically handcuffed him to the metal scaffolding that stood at one side, and exited at the rear of the hall without saying a word. It was a clear, forceful, somewhat brutal image quite in keeping with Paik's style. I wondered where he had found his three well-drilled assistants.

Nam June was calling feebly but only half-intelligibly about his inability to get to the piano when the chimpanzee's owner and trainer appeared behind me. "Your friend needs help," he said, motioning toward the back of the building. "He's got those guys trapped." He was referring to George Pappaniko-laou, who had been helping with production work. Realizing that the handcuffing had not been Paik's invention, I ran to the back door.

George was guarding the door. "They're out there," he said, "and they can't get away. It's locked downstairs." The exit opened onto a metal fire escape that extended from the ground to the roof. Leaving the chimp's owner to watch the door, we went out to find the three men. The door at the bottom of the twisting staircase was locked, as George knew from the com-ments he had heard when the three rushed down. But the men were not there. Obviously, they had gone up to the roof. I went up. The fire escape, walled by heavy railings and bars, did not allow access to the roof, but the three men were not there, either. Although the door leading back into the theatre was the only way out of the enclosed staircase, they had disappeared. We wondered what to do about Nam June, handcuffed to the scaffolding. Then I saw a narrow ladder leading to another level and a water tower and knew they must be there.

It is not true that, as Jill Johnston reported, "One of them was later found to be stuck head down in an apparatus on the roof." The three were standing quietly against the wall by the tank. They came down docilely but would not speak or give us the key to the handcuffs. I had never seen them before. One finally gave his name. He was lying: It was the name of an acquaintance, and now we knew who had put them up to the stunt. I rushed back to the performance. The fellow I was looking for had been there but had left, perhaps taking the key with him. The three were beginning to talk a little, admitting that they were students on their way back to Johns Hopkins, when the police arrived.

It was somewhat difficult to explain to the policemen about the performance and the handcuffing. They seemed a little confused but tolerant. Then Paik arrived, upset, agitated, and sweating. He had been freed. One of the policemen became very righteous and indignant about the marks on Nam June's wrists, but Paik wouldn't press charges, and the three students had a police escort out to Fifty-seventh Street. All of us remember the incident, I suppose, with a certain kind of pleasure—all except, perhaps, Nam June Paik. And the spectators may have thought, as I did at first, that it was all part of the performance.

The Uses
of Film
in the
New Theatre

The film experience is not necessarily a single rectangle of light and shadow that flickers at one end of a darkened room. Call this "movies" or "cinema"—that archetypal dream world in which the spectator, seated in a near-foetal position, attempts to ignore the physical space, the other spectators, the projector's shifting beam, to concentrate on the images and the sounds that accompany them. Of course, the movies are a film experience—and a theatre experience—but the use of motion pictures is not so limited, and theatre is just beginning to realize the possibilities inherent in film.

For many years, motion pictures have been used as elements in staged drama—epic and "total" theatre, the "living newspaper," etc. In 1941, Robert Edmund Jones foresaw "in the

simultaneous use of the living actor and the talking picture
. . . a wholly new theatrical art, whose possibilities are as
infinite as those of speech itself." [1] But it seems that Jones confused "drama" and "theatre," making them synonymous, and
the single example of this "wholly new theatrical art" which he
gave was no more of an innovation than O'Neill's use of masks:
"Some new playwright will presently set a motion-picture
screen on the stage above and behind his actors and will reveal
simultaneously the two worlds of the conscious and the unconscious. . . ." [2] I mention this to emphasize that I am not
going to write about plays; however, Jones's general prophecy
has come true, and I shall concentrate on recent performances
which, by using film in new ways, have shown formal alternatives to both traditional movies and traditional theatre.

The earliest systematic challenge to orthodox film experience was made by the German Bauhaus of the 1920's. Employing modern science and technology for artistic ends, the work
of the Bauhaus prefigured many recent developments. Farkas
Molnar's U-Theatre, Andreas Weininger's Spherical Theatre,
and Walter Gropius' Total Theatre were all unrealized theoretical attempts to break away from the simple axial confronta-
tion of spectator and proscenium arch or motion picture screen.
By presenting film, light, and performance images to the observer from various angles and distances, the Bauhaus artists
hoped to create a more complex and—as underlined by their
writing—more profound theatrical experience. Moholy-Nagy
proposed replacing the traditional movie screen and its conno-
tation of the picture frame with convex or concave screens
of different sizes and shapes: in one 1924 version, three films
were to be projected simultaneously onto the inner surface of
a hemisphere. In his *Malerei, Photographie, Film,* published
in Germany in 1925, and in *Vision in Motion,* published here
in 1961, he suggests that different films—one assumes, knowing
his line of thought, that they would be more abstract than

[1] Robert Edmund Jones, *The Dramatic Imagination* (New York:
Theatre Arts Books, 1965), p. 17.

[2] *Ibid.,* p. 18.

narrative—be projected simultaneously onto the walls of the auditorium.

In 1953 I saw a demonstration by Jim Davis of one of his abstract light devices. Basically a hanging sculpture made from variously colored pieces of plastic, it reflected moving patterns of colored light onto the walls, ceiling, and floor of the room when a light was beamed onto it. Davis, a painter who gave up painting because "everything has been done," used the mobiles and the light patterns they created as the raw material for nonobjective films in which he had more control over the relationship between the swirls of color and their accompanying music. Another early attempt at "environmental" projection effects—"early," that is, in terms of the relatively great amount of activity in the last year or so—was Al Hansen's contribution to *The Ray Gun Spex* program at Judson Church in New York in late February and early March, 1960. Several hand-held projectors moved film images at varying rates across all four walls and the ceiling. As I remember, the pictures were mostly of airplanes and of parachutists. At times they would overlap or chase each other or the picture would be stopped so that the heat of the projection lamp melted the film, creating a different kind of moving image.

One of those who has worked longest and most consistently on a form of environmental projection theatre is Milton Cohen, who teaches art at the University of Michigan. Since 1958, he has been developing what he calls "Space Theatre," with the help of other members of the ONCE group: Harold Borkin, George Manupelli, Robert Ashley, and Gordon Mumma. The heart of the Space Theatre is a system of rotating, adjustable mirrors and prisms that can project light, slides, or motion picture images in any direction—either onto a dome or onto screens surrounding and above the spectators. The earliest presentations combined fluid, shifting abstract color patterns with music; later, the "palette" was broadened to include "hard-edge" forms, recognizable images, and even human performers.

Cohen has built a permanent but constantly modified Space Theatre in the loft where he lives in Ann Arbor. Triangular screens attached to the walls and ceilings in various places face the battery of projectors and the rotating reflection equipment in the center of the room. The spectators sit or recline on cushions, moving and turning to view the images that appear around them. In one of his more recent performances, various textures, patterns, geometrical figures, and realistic pictures were produced by the central equipment in a planned sequence. A girl wearing a costume distended in a dehumanizing way by balloons performed simple movements at one side of the room, a red light within her costume going on and off at various times. Films of the same girl and of Cohen himself, who was visible as he operated the projection equipment, were flashed onto the screens. A "musical" accompaniment was produced by amplifying the sounds of the projectors and the reflecting mechanism. A recent addition to Cohen's Space Theatre is an adjustable screen or, more accurately, a series of screens made up of square perforated panels hinged one above the other to two vertical poles. The panels can be pivoted at various times during the performance so that the images falling upon them are fractured by the combination of angled surfaces. When light from the projectors passes through the holes in the screens, photoelectric cells are activated, producing a kind of "noise music."

From the first, Happenings have used projections as separate elements in the performance. John Cage's presentation at Black Mountain College in the summer of 1952 combined a film projected on the ceiling and walls with readings, music, and dance. One part of Allan Kaprow's eponymous *18 Happenings in 6 Parts* (1959) was a series of slide projections; shadows were thrown on a scrim in Red Groom's *The Magic Train Ride* (1960), etc. Perhaps the happener who has done the most consistent and elaborate work with films is Robert Whitman, a sculptor who uses motion pictures in his plastic works as well as in his performances. During the First New York Theatre Rally (1965), he exhibited a real shower stall. It actually worked, and water could be heard inside and seen on a closed translucent curtain on which was projected the life-sized image of a girl taking a shower. Although the water in the film changed color and closeups of the shower head and of the colored water running over bare skin were inserted, some viewers apparently thought the girl, too, might be real. During some "Expanded Cinema" presentations sponsored in 1965 by the Film-Makers' Cinemathèque, Whitman exhibited a dressing table, the "mirror" of which was a rear-projection device showing, as if it were the reflection, a girl carefully applying variously colored skin creams: she became blue, red, green, while now a river, now a city street, now trees were seen behind her.

In Whitman's *The American Moon* (1960) the audience watched the performance from six enclosures that radiated from a central playing space. At one point, sheets of plastic partly covered with rows of paper rectangles were lowered over each opening, and projectors at the rear of each tunnel beamed the same film onto these mosaic screens. When the lights were out in the central space, the spectators could see through the transparent plastic that separated the pieces of paper and watch, from the rear, the film being projected in the opposite tunnel. The basic images of the film—cloth-covered mounds and balls that moved in various ways—were repeated and echoed during several other parts of the presentation. In *Water* (1963), in which a girl appeared in front of various film pictures of herself, Whitman again compared a real performance image with its projected version. He later carried this basic technique—perhaps *the* basic principle of most performance-film pieces—to a high degree of elaboration in the recent *Prune Flat* (1965). Unlike almost all of his previous Happenings, *Prune Flat* was presented from the stage of a traditional theatre. Upstage, a projection screen stretching the entire width of the stage was filled by the filmed activities of two girls while the same girls performed in person in front of the screen. A third girl wearing a long white dress was also on stage. The dress acted as a screen to receive her own life-sized color film image, and her movements were synchronized with those projected. For example, the film alter ego undressed at one point while the real girl went through the same motions—"throwing" her coat into the wings, stepping out of her skirt, etc.—without, of course, ever removing the white "screen" dress. At the end of the sequence, a life-sized nude image of the girl was projected on her own fully-clothed figure. During the performance, connections were continually made between the film and live images; when the "disrobing" girl threw her (filmed) coat into the wings, for example, one of the other two girls appeared wearing the real coat.

Another artist who deserves mention for his pioneering work in what he calls Filmstage—the combination of film and live performance—is the actor Roberts Blossom. One of his earliest examples of Filmstage, in 1961, was a piece written by Stephen Tropp. Two or three very large cardboard boxes could be seen on the stage behind a scrim; while a film of the ocean was projected on the scrim, soft sporadic noises could be heard coming from the boxes, and they moved slightly. More recently, Blossom has combined live dancing with films of the same dance, using synchronization, counterpoint, and closeup—a dance passage is remembered from the preceding film images or vice versa, a large foot fills the screen and performs the same movements as that of the real dancer. In one piece a sudden transition from black-and-white film to a brightly colored slide coincides with a costume change the dancer makes, causing an abrupt transition of tempo and mood. In another piece, the use of negative film adds another dimension to the comparison of real performer and her "unreal" film images.

While all these works use motion pictures taken particularly for the performance, *Unmarked Interchange* by the ONCE group is an example of the use of "found" film—film from another source that was not intended to be part of such a presentation. When *Unmarked Interchange* was performed at the ONCE AGAIN 1965 festival, a screen resembling that of a drive-in movie was erected on the flat roof of an Ann Arbor parking garage. While the Fred Astaire–Ginger Rogers film *Top Hat* was projected on it, sliding panels, louvers, and a large drawer-like section that moved out were manipulated to combine live performers inside and in front of the screen with the Hollywood images. Behind an opening in the upper right corner of the screen, for example, a man, his voice amplified, read excerpts from the modern pornographic classic *The Story of O,* while at intervals a girl crossed a narrow catwalk in front of the screen from a similar opening near the opposite top corner and threw custard pies in his face. Behind another opening, a man played a small piano. A man and a woman sat at a table, dining formally by candlelight on the drawer-like section that moved out in front of the screen. The system of large vertical louvers stretching more than halfway across the center of the screen was opened at various angles and lit from behind to reveal girls hanging laundry, attaching large silhouette drawings of the human figure to the movable clotheslines, etc. As live sounds were added to those of the sound track, the images of *Top Hat* were increasingly faceted by the live performers, the props, and the various sections of opening, louver, and backing, each of which became a particular kind of subsidiary screen reflecting parts of the main picture and mixing with it.

These examples of uses of the motion picture in performance are from the New Theatre, but similar examples are available from quite a different source—the recent New York World's Fair. Film was everywhere at the fair, and although in many cases its use was quite traditional, in others it was used in ways very much like those of the New Theatre. As might be expected in a "world of the future," several of the pavilions reflected two dominant facets of recent theatrical thought: manipulation of the audience-presentation relationship and use of film as one element of a performance composed of many elements.

At the New York State pavilion, the spectator stood in a large circular hall about 100 feet in diameter. Eight contiguous movie screens, each the size of the average wide cinemascope screen, formed a continuous band around the hall. Since the bottom of this huge composite screen was about ten feet above the floor, all parts of it could be seen with relative ease from any point. The audience was limited in size, and the spectator was free to walk about during the performance. The color

film—actually eight separate films which were usually synchronized to form a continuous image around the audience—
put the spectator in the center of the visual experience rather
than leaving him outside the rectangular window of the traditional movie. He traveled along a road in a car or down a river
in a canoe, with the road or river moving toward him at one
side of the hall and away from him on the other, while the
landscape slid by on either side. Or he was in the center of a
hockey game with the opposing goalies and their nets projected at opposite sides and the puck being passed back and
forth "across" the hall as the players surged one way and then
the other. Or he "stood formation" with military cadets, some
figures looming huge in closeup while other platoons were
drawn up farther away as the reports of the unit leaders came
from various parts of the screen. (The films were all real scenes
taken in New York State, but one cannot help imagining what
the traditional Western would look like in this format—the
Indians riding around the audience as well as around the de-
fensive circle of covered wagons; the hero strolling under the
prairie stars with the heroine at one side while at the other side,
in the distance, a band of outlaws ride into town to rob the
bank.)

The "World of Chemistry" show at the DuPont pavilion did
not alter the traditional audience-presentation relationship: the
audience was seated facing the stage of a small theatre to
watch a show for which Michael Brown wrote the words and
music. But film was only one of the performance elements.
Three plain rectangular boxes, each about the size of the average door and perhaps a foot thick, moved on and off stage
without any visible means of locomotion, along tracks in the
stage floor parallel to the proscenium arch. At times all three
boxes would join together to form one wide projection screen;
at other times the screen would be two boxes wide. Live actors
played scenes with films projected on the mechanically shifted
screens: the master of ceremonies "blew out" a projected candle, an actress ordered food from a film grocer, etc. At one
point the three screen units were separated, the life-sized image

of a dancing girl was projected on each, and two real men danced the same steps in the intervals between the screens. Then the filmed girl at stage left handed a rose to the real man on her right, and the rose, alternately real and on film, passed down the line of dancers. (As the live dancer reached behind the screen box to pick up or deposit a real rose, the image of "his" hand reached into the film image at exactly the same point to take or deliver the rose.)

In the show created by Charles Eames at the IBM pavilion, the spectators walked up a complicated system of wide wooden stairs and filed into a steel structure in which they half-stood, half-sat in narrow rows, each row rising quite a bit above the one behind it so that everyone could see easily. A formally dressed master of ceremonies descended on a small platform from the ceiling in front of this somewhat compressed and steeply raked version of the traditional theatre seating arrangement, and told the spectators what was about to happen. Then the whole audience unit began to rise upward and backward at a forty-five-degree angle, sliding slowly and smoothly on giant steel tracks. From perhaps thirty feet below the master of ceremonies, passersby watched the audience section, holding about 500 people, move up into the huge ovoid dome of the pavilion: those who were about to see the performance inside the dome became part of the "performance" for other spectators. Once the carrier stopped inside the dome, large doors closed under it. The audience now faced one broad curving inner face of the dome where sixteen projection screens, mostly rectangular but of different sizes, were spaced in an asymmetrical arrangement. Both still and motion pictures were projected on the multiple screens. At times all of the screens were in use; at other times only a few had images on them. An auto race, for example, was shown from the grandstands, from the track, from the driver's seat, from inside the engine—all at the same moment. Or the steps in a woman's thoughts as she planned a dinner party were shown by images appearing and disappearing on various screens—the single faces of the guests, the seating plan, the table itself, etc. At times the spectator "read" a spatially distributed sequence of images, his eyes moving in an intended sequence from one screen to another; at others he could not look at each of the simultaneous projections, and the choice of where to focus was his own. The master of ceremonies appeared now and then standing precipitously between the screens or in the shallow space revealed when a screen was raised, to comment on and explain the pictures. When the film part of the performance ended, the huge doors opened and the "people-wall" slid slowly down to its starting position, where the spectators filed off, and a new audience was loaded aboard.

These performances indicate the range of possibilities in the theatrical use of motion pictures. Projected imagery varies from nonobjective or abstract to figurative, from fantasy to documentary; various types of imagery are combined in the same piece. Slide, overhead, and opaque projectors are combined with film projectors of all kinds and sizes. Multiple screens provide the audience with different viewing angles, and simultaneous presentation of images or 360-degree projection forces the viewer to make perceptual choices. The whole hemisphere above "ground level"—and more—becomes available to receive pictures, while the viewer sits, stands, moves about, lies down. Three-dimensional and movable screens, human and inanimate, are used. And the projections are combined with every other performance material—actors, dancers, music, etc.—in various proportions and combinations.

There is a primary difference between the performances given at the World's Fair and those which I have called part of the New Theatre. The New Theatre is made up of individual artists pursuing more or less personal and subjective aesthetic goals. The theatre that Milton Cohen has constructed in his own living loft shows that theatrical creativity is possible at almost the same level of privacy as that enjoyed by the painter, sculptor, or writer. For the most part, the artists of the New Theatre are working for a relatively small audience that is well aware of the traditions on which the work is based. (The fact that a group, ONCE, is included among the "individual" artists in no way alters my point. As a group, their style, approach, and theories are as clear and recognizable as are the personal concerns of Milton Cohen, for example, who is also one of the group. Conversely, the aesthetic sympathies and inclinations necessary for complete appreciation of ONCE— Dada, Surrealism, theatre of the absurd, Pop—are distinct from the background to which Cohen's Space Theatre refers: Bauhaus, abstract expressionism, Symbolism. Although the actual audiences overlap, the theoretical audiences for which these artists work are discrete and, because they depend upon artistic sophistication, small.)

Although the performances at the World's Fair were frequently conceived by individuals, the "target" was a mass audience. They exploited differences between their work and the play or movie familiar to everyone, but the imagery and intellectual references were limited to the material of that same theatre and of everyday life. (To say this is, of course, not qualitative criticism.) The limited audiences for which the New Theatre seems intended come from almost all artistic disciplines. Those who work with film in the New Theatre are sculptors, painters, dancers, musicians, and filmmakers; appreciation of their theatre work requires somewhat the same sensibilities that are needed to appreciate their other work. Strangely enough, Roberts Blossom is one of the few professional actors or directors working in the New Theatre, and it is perhaps this use of unfamiliar aesthetic attitudes that has prevented many theatre people from becoming involved in any way with the new work.

The meaning of the theatrical elements used in the new work depends more upon the relationship of each element to the others than it does upon the character of the image itself. A totally abstract image such as a projection of shifting amorphous yellow light may exist only in its sensory dimensions when related to nonobjective material, but it may also be seen as a "warning signal," "reflection from the water," "ghost," etc., when set in a context that generates cognitive meanings. At the other extreme, a completely recognizable image may create little "meaning" when placed next to abstract material: the film image of a girl on a beach in Cohen's Space Theatre, for example, does not carry the same information in its juxtaposition with geometrical shapes and fractured pictures as it would in a story which explained who the girl was, why she was on the beach, which beach it was, etc.

Traditional and almost all avant-garde theatre make use of an *information structure:* the images and scenes pass information back and forth to increase the intellectual density of each. Whether or not the events are presented in the "proper" sequence, a story structure (of which plot is a heightened form) is usually followed. But story should not be thought of as synonymous with information structure. Although two of the World's Fair shows included story segments juxtaposed with other elements, none of them had a plot. Instead, a narrator or master of ceremonies linked one element to another: the result was a "package" in both the industrial and theatrical sense. For example, the DuPont production combined a short history of plastics (story) and a fashion show (in a song-and-dance format) with no intellectual incongruity.[3]

Of course, every image can be perceived as "containing" information—the Rorschach inkblots show this. Unfortunately, many people are so used to finding meaning in theatre that they look for it even when the artist does not intend it. Confronting works without information structures, audiences ask, "What does it mean?" or project a meaning, or say the piece is "absurd" and philosophize on the "meaning of meaninglessness." But meaning and significance are not synonymous. Great significance may be perceived in a work that does not intend to communicate meaning (lacks an information structure). A performance can be totally abstract. Of course, there is such a

[3] For an example of an information structure based on neither chronology nor the verbal "frame" see *The First and Second Wilderness* in "Performance Chronology," pp. 172-77.

thing as the "Rorschach fallacy's" reverse in which an audience perceives images as purely sensory even when there is clear meaning intended. Meaning and abstraction form a continuum and they may be mixed in varying proportions. To seek one extreme or the other in every case is often to miss the quality of the artwork.

It should also be understood that actions, representations, and objects can exist for their own sake and not as conveyors of meaning. Information elements (such as objects, actions, and so forth) do not contribute to a cumulative meaning when they are isolated in a complex performance structure. Even if every line, shape, and color is thought to have an unconscious symbolic meaning (our yellow light or Cohen's geometrical figures, for example) one can easily see that the complicated *relationships* that make up many works would confute any overall information structure one might care to construct.

A dense spectrum of possibilities exists between the poles of information structure and abstract or alogical structure. The World's Fair productions that I have described lie somewhat closer to the alogical end of the scale than does most traditional theatre: at IBM, the operation of the "people-wall" was completely separate from the informative aspects; at DuPont, the rose which passed back and forth between film and three-dimensional existence was not "explained" and did not "send" information to any other part of the performance. At the New York State pavilion, the presentation gained reality from the 360-degree projection, but nothing was added to the message. Here the alogical or purely formal elements are more unrelated to the information structure than they are in traditional theatre, but the information structure still dominates. In the New Theatre, on the other hand, informative connections may appear here and there, but relationships of another order predominate.

Thus an examination of a few of the large number of recent theatrical productions using film indicates some of the possibilities. This is only a beginning: the future will show increased investigation of all forms of projection, their relationship to the spectator, their relationship to other performance materials. As more sculptures and paintings use film, more theatre people and filmmakers will find in their own studio theatres the privacy of the sculptor and the painter. The limits of this new theatre are only those of science and imagination.

ART AND TECHNOLOGY

The *Nine Evenings: Theatre and Engineering* program, co-sponsored in October, 1966, by Experiments in Art and Technology, Inc. and The Foundation for Contemporary Performance Arts, Inc., was probably the most elaborate and expensive presentation of avant-garde performances ever attempted in this country. With an impressive list of backers and patrons, months of preparation and quite a bit of rather lurid publicity, the productions were staged at the same huge armory on Twenty-fifth Street in New York that had housed the famous Armory Show responsible for introducing European avant-garde painting to this country in 1913. The cost of renting the armory would, in itself, have paid for any number of performances on the scale to which the participants had been accustomed. The total budget was, to some, staggering. Steve Paxton wanted identical twins in his piece, and promised that my brother's transportation would twice be paid to and from Bennington, Vermont, so that he and I could stand in Paxton's inflated plastic Environment.

Robert Rauschenberg used a huge "cast" in his piece, *Open Score*. In the second section, perhaps 300 people were photographed in complete darkness by infrared television cameras; their images as they performed certain simple actions on cue were projected on three large hanging screens. The first time the piece was done, a tape recording was played on which people, one after the other, simply said, "My name is _____." giving their names. When the piece was repeated nine days later, the tape was not used. After the performance I told Bob I liked it much better without the tape. "I didn't," he said, "but when I got here this evening, I found that one of the engineers had accidentally erased the whole thing."

Environmental Theatre

The medieval theatre-in-the-round made use of raised acting platforms at various spots around the circumference of its circular enclosure as well as employing a central acting space and the radial aisles through the audience. Apparently the arrangement and number of the peripheral towers varied according to the needs of the particular play. In *The Seven Ages of the Theatre*, Richard Southern tells us of an amazing French script, *The Play of the Leafed One,* written by Adam de la Hale in 1276 to be staged in front of the pub in Arras. It not only made use of the real inn, yard, and streets as "setting," but the names of the author and other townspeople were used for "characters" in the play, and actors on stage talked with actors in the audience.

In general, however, we can say that environmental theatre is a recent development. The design of traditional stages is basically functional. It is a practical solution to the problem of presenting a certain type of theatrical material to audiences of various sizes and social characteristics. Even illusionistic developments such as Wagner's "mystic gulf" apply to a type of theatre rather than to individual theatrical works. Environmental theatre, on the other hand, can be viewed as a way in which the spatial characteristics of the stage itself as it is related to the spectator may become a specific aesthetic element of a particular presentation. Environmental theatre, in this sense, makes use of an expressive dimension that is not exploited by traditional performance arrangements.

Two somewhat different meanings of the word "environmental" may be distinguished: one abstract and theoretical, the other concrete and practical. The former is based on pure spatial considerations, while the latter refers to various types of theatre outside of theatres. Taking the more general concept first, we have the definition of "environment" as "the surrounding" and "that which encircles, encompasses." The compass gives us names for every possible point on the horizontal plane that extends away from us in every direction; thus, assuming the traditionally seated spectator, we may say that any theatre is environmental if it presents material from the sides and rear of the viewer as well as from the front.

An annular or ring stage completely surrounding the audience is the simplest model for this concept of environmental theatre. When Guillaume Apollinaire added a prologue to his *The Breasts of Tiresias* in 1916, he indicated that rather than the "antique stage" that was being used for the performance he would have preferred "A circular theatre with two stages / One in the middle the other like a ring / Around the spectators . . . " This would have allowed "The full unfolding of our modern art."

Several stages that completely surround the audience have been constructed. One example is the Waco Civic Theatre, a project of James Hull Miller, who has been very active in proselytizing for more flexible and environmental theatre design. The somewhat egg-shaped seating section, flattened at one end where it faces the primary playing area, is sunk below the level of the main floor so that a continuous peripheral stage actually surrounds it. The 360-degree stage is horizontal, as in our theoretical model.

If the central seating section in this type of arrangement is raked, however, to provide a better view toward the front, sight lines to the side and rear become a problem. One solution is to surround the spectators with motion picture screens that can be hung high enough so that they can be seen easily by everyone. At the New York State pavilion at the recent World's Fair in New York and in an exhibition produced by Walt Disney for Expo 67, contiguous cinemascope screens ringed the circular "auditorium," and synchronized films presented a "single" continuous image within which the spectator was centered. The well-known but unrealized "Total Theatre" that Walter Gropius designed for Erwin Piscator in 1926 also used projection screens to enclose an audience completely. Thomas Wilfred's "Heptarena" is a similar but more intimate concept using front projection rather than rear projection. Both of these proposed theatres were conceived to extend the scenery ("backdrop") of a play environmentally: In each the physical staging can be varied from proscenium through thrust stage to arena, but the audience is always within the ring of projected setting.

Where live actors are concerned, a solution to the sight-line problem of a raked seating section is to raise the side and rear portions of the surrounding stage. The Nationaltheater in Mannheim, Germany, which uses elevated side aisles as stages, and the Hilberry Classic Theatre at Wayne State University in Detroit, Michigan, in which a stepped metal ramp surrounds the audience, are two examples of this approach.

This elevation of side and rear stages suggests that our simple theoretical model of a horizontal plane extending away from the spectator in all directions is not the most useful one for environmental theatre: the purest archetype is a sphere with the individual spectator at its center. The stimuli that make up the performance may now come from any three-dimensional direction, and, rather than merely the points of the compass referring to the horizontal plane, we now have all the points on a sphere for reference.

Because of the expense and technical difficulties of suspending the individual spectator in space, a "pure" architectural realization of this theoretical model has not yet been built. Frederick Kiesler's "Endless Theatre," designed in 1924, was a huge flattened sphere with a double outer wall of glass or plastic. The architect described his project as "the first continuous shell construction with no foundation to support it." (In many respects it can be compared with Andreas Weininger's proposed "Spherical Theatre," the concept for which was also published in Germany in 1924.) Kiesler's theatre had great flexibility. Permanent seats ringed the shell at its widest point, and lower seats also surrounded a central arena, but that half of the structure above the heads of the audience, the huge smooth dome, could serve as a continuous projection screen. There were three permanent stages in the "Endless Theatre": a round stage in the center of the arena, and two squarish platform stages that broke the lower ring of seats at either side. Bridges could join the side stages with the central stage. From the very top of the dome, a platform for carrying actors could be raised and lowered; elevators could be positioned anywhere in the space. And great adjustable spiral ramps, inclining at various angles, could be suspended within the shell. (Kiesler pointed out that the "elastic building system of cables and platforms developed from bridge building.") These ramps, rising to a ring stage suspended near the top of the dome, could be used either for the audience—hanging them, in some arrangements, in the very center of the space—or for performance. Or both audience and performance could occupy sections of the same spiral "road." Like so many of his projects, the "Endless Theatre" was never constructed, but Kiesler was allowed to erect a "double spiral stage" in the Vienna Concert House for the Music and Theatre Festival in 1924.

More recently, Jacques Polieri has proposed spherical theatres. In his "Théâtre du mouvement total," small seating sections for spectators are to be inserted into the center of a
huge sphere. The performance is to take place on the inner
surface of the sphere and within it. In one concept the audience is seated on the "blades" of paddle-like extensions from
a central core; in another the platforms are raised on tall metal
stalks.

Since the space beneath the spectator is the most difficult
to deal with from a practical point of view, we can find examples of "spherical" thought that have been realized only as
domes over the audience. In a very small spherical theatre in
the French pavilion at Expo 67, a specially photographed film
was projected onto a mirror that focused the image onto most
of the dome-shaped surface around the spectators and over
their heads. The "Space Theatre" that Milton Cohen has built
in Ann Arbor, Michigan, roughly approximates a hemisphere
by hanging screens for film projection above and around the
spectators. *The Night Time Sky* (1965) by Robert Whitman
set several small elevated "stages" into the walls of a roughly
dome-shaped tentlike enclosure. Elements of the performance
also took place on the main floor among the spectators, who
were free to move about or recline on mats, and films were
projected at various spots in the enclosure, including directly
overhead.

Many Happenings have approximated conceptually our
spherical environmental model by using for the performance
all of the available three-dimensional space, including that
occupied by the spectators. In this respect at least, they had
a great influence on discothèques. Although I do not consider discothèques as art, they are an example of environmental
concern that is widely available and with which many people
are familiar. Such an obvious stereotype exists for the light-
show discothèque that it is not necessary to name any particular example: projections of various sorts are directed onto
the walls, floor, ceiling, and onto the dancers themselves. Other
points that make the discothèque worth mentioning are the

way in which the volume of the amplified music often seems to "fill" the entire space and the way the individual dancer becomes the center of experience. The kinesthetic and proprioceptive basis of dancing for pleasure rather than to be seen emphasizes the spherical model with a single spectator as its center, in contrast to the consideration of the audience as an undifferentiated mass.

But the spherical archetype is not intended to be taken literally. Being a hypothetical construct, it can "fit" any theatre and any space and serve as a measure of the degree of environmental involvement. Thus it is only when the presentational field and/or performance elements move around, over, or under the spectator that we may call the performance "environmental." From this point of view, thrust and arena staging are not significantly different from proscenium. The spectator sees each from one fixed angle. Of course the visual angle taken up by the stage is inversely related to the viewer's distance from the performance: The visual angle is much greater, for example, for a person in the front row than it is for someone thirty rows back. Nevertheless, all traditional audience-stage relationships are, from the point of view of the individual spectator, *frontal*. Once this basic principle is established, we find that stages actually exist that enclose the spectator to various degrees: "side" or "end" stages move around the auditorium in a variety of ways, "caliper" stages grip the audience between them, and so forth. Since we are involved with a continuum, there is nothing to be gained by specifying the exact angular deviation at which "frontal" theatre becomes "environmental," but the spherical construct indicates tendency toward environmental staging as clearly as it represents the extreme examples of the form.

Since any place, theatrical or not, can be examined in terms of our spherical model, the important point is whether or not the sensations coming to the spectator are intrinsic, functioning parts of the performance. These spatial elements may be purely abstract, utilizing the different qualities and characteristics of various viewing angles, for example, or they may relate more literally to the atmosphere or information structure of the presentation.

When *A Sleep of Prisoners* by Christopher Fry is presented, as it often is, in an actual church, the total physical surroundings of the audience are obviously related to the particular piece being presented: The spectator is in the "church turned into a prison camp" for which the script calls. Every element of the real church is justified by the play and becomes a part of it. The spectator is "spherically" involved by the architecture. In this case, the involvement is passive, but the performance, even when the director chooses to place all of the action in a quasi-proscenium arrangement near the altar, therefore can be considered to have an environmental attribute or dimension.

The same kind of passive, physical, environmental involvement exists if a play is presented as being "set" in a theatre. From Pirandello to Peter Weiss we have attempts to use the actual environment of the spectator and integrate it into the intellectual and emotional fabric of the work. The scripts of *Six Characters* and *Marat/Sade* do not call for any active involvement of the audience by the actors, but the spectator is physically "included" in the work, nevertheless.

A slightly more difficult way to achieve this kind of passive architectural involvement is to build a complete enclosure for the audience, extending the setting so that it surrounds the seating section much as the projection screens in Gropius' and Wilfred's proposed theatres would do. When Max Reinhardt staged *The Miracle*, the whole interior of the theatre was turned into an Early Gothic cathedral with tall pillars and arches and huge stained glass windows; when the performance came to this country, Norman Bel Geddes was responsible for the conversion of New York's Century Theatre into a "total setting."

Of course in a play these passive environmental techniques are related to the "suspension of disbelief." We are asked to equate the real church we may perhaps know from our everyday life with the unreal (acted) soldiers, for example. Whether or not this makes the tangible world somehow less real or merely makes the performers seem more artificial depends upon the spectator. And even with the complete integration of the architectural space into the play, it is possible that another physical element will be omitted: the audience. During the performance, the church in *A Sleep of Prisoners* is obviously not empty, as it is represented by the dialogue. The clothes I wear as I watch the Marquis de Sade on the stage of a nineteen-century mental institution obviously belong to a different time.

In alogical theatre, which does not involve such elaborate use of informational cross-reference, many performances have been presented in complete Environments designed and constructed for the particular piece. Allan Kaprow's *18 Happenings in 6 Parts* took place simultaneously in three adjoining plastic-walled rooms; the spectators changed seats during the two intermissions. A standing audience watched Kaprow's *A Spring Happening* through narrow slits in the side walls of a long "boxcar." In Robert Whitman's *The American Moon,* spectators sat in six tunnels facing a central playing space. Jim Dine's *The Car Crash* enclosed the audience in a completely white Environment: The performers also wore white, and Dine even considered giving the spectators white caps and smocks to wear in order to integrate them with the space.

Of course the environmental aspects of most performances are physically active rather than passive. The aisles, lobbies, and balconies of traditional theatres are used by performers in many different ways. When the spectator is considered to be at the center of a hypothetical sphere, the rest of the audience is part of his "environment," and the device of having actors "planted" as spectators and performing from the house itself rather than from the stage can be seen as an environmental concern. It was used in André Antoine's production of *Le Missionaire* in 1894, in the surrealist *The Mysteries of Love* by Roger Vitrac directed by Antonin Artaud in 1927, in *Waiting for Lefty,* and *The Case of Clyde Griffiths* of the 1930's, among many others.

(Although the concept of "audience involvement" is usually employed in discussing the use of the spectators' area for acting purposes, the terminology is tricky. I have been using the word "involvement" in an objective, physical sense, and there is, of course, greater *physical* involvement for the spectator in all environmental theatre: turning to see the actors behind him, for example, is a basically physical act. But physical involvement should not be equated with or misunderstood as *psychological* involvement. It should be obvious that a spectator seated in a top balcony at some spatial remove from the actual performance can be absolutely involved in a psychological sense while, on the other hand, a spectator physically surrounded by a performance or even participating in it may have no psychological involvement at all.)

In environmental theatre the particular three-dimensional spatial relationship between the performance element and the spectator tends to have particular significance in an intellectual or purely plastic sense. Some of the more obvious possibilities of the intellectual use of spatial dynamics, for example, were embodied in the first section of the Canadian National Film Board's "Labyrinth" at Montreal's Expo 67. Spectators stood on four galleries curving along each side of an ovoid space and watched films projected on two huge rectangular screens, one rising vertically at one end of the large room and the other stretching across the floor below. The sensation of looking *down* onto a film was unique and, for many, disconcerting. Feelings of uneasiness were played upon by the authors of the piece with colorful vertiginous action: moving aerial shots; sky divers falling through space; boys climbing an unfinished skyscraper on the vertical screen, while on the horizonal screen the drop to the streets below becomes longer and longer. In Jacques Polieri's *Gamme de 7*, on the other hand, the relationship to dancers seen from beneath the transparent platform on which they are performing is purely a formal one, unrelated to information.

Although a complete documentation of all the possibilities

of environmental theatre is not intended here, a description of certain key works and directors can indicate historical progression as well as diversity of approach.

As has already been mentioned, Reinhardt staged *The Miracle*, a wordless play by Karl Vollmoeller, in theatre auditoriums and exhibition halls that had been completely transformed into a cathedral. But there was active as well as passive environmental involvement in *The Miracle*. The *regie book* for the presentation is filled with movement in the aisles, and action takes place in all parts of the space. As The Nun flees into the auditorium in Scene V, for example, "Everywhere black shadows step in front of her." Although the performers did not speak, sound was an important element in the performance, and this, too, was treated environmentally, as indicated in the following passages from the production outline.

SCENE 2

31. The Piper then tiptoes to the front and calls as if up into the hills with a mooselike cry.

32. The answer is heard coming from the upper gallery, then the middle one, and soon the lower one.

33. The blowing of horns, the barking of hounds . . .

SCENE 3

43. Whispering comes from all parts of the church. High crackling laughter.

. . .

65. The Nun shrieks, but only makes the formation of her mouth; the sound comes from the gallery.

SCENE 5

265. There is a strong menacing knock at one of the doors of the auditorium.

. . .

268. The knocking is repeated in always shorter intervals with increasing vehemence.

269. Finally it resounds from all the doors round about and ends at last in a mighty, growing, threatening thunder.

In February, 1923, Vsevolod Meyerhold staged a play adapted by Sergei Tretyakov from *The Night* by Marcel Martinet, the title of which is variously translated as *The Earth Rises, Earth on Its Hind Legs,* or *The Restive Earth.* "Audience participation" apparently began before the performance itself, when waiting spectators took part in organized marching in the lobby. During the presentation—which was set during the Civil War and employed soldiers whose full battle equipment included small cannon—cars, trucks, motorcycles, and bicycles drove through the auditorium and to and from the stage across a bridge. Finally, according to René Fülöp-Miller. the Red troops arrived, took possession of "the stage, the auditorium and the foyer," and the spectators stood while everyone sang the *Internationale.*

In the late 1930's Nikolai Okhlopkov presented several productions at the Realistic Theatre in Moscow that made radical and programmatic use of environmental factors. Having at his disposal a small rectangular theatre hall with a flat floor, a balcony at one end, and a low platform stage at the other, Okhlopkov ignored the direct frontal relationship between audience and performance for which the space had been designed. For each production he created a new and particular arrangement of seats and playing areas, surrounding the audience with the action in various ways.

For *The Start* by Vasili Stavsky (also translated as *The Run*) the audience sat in two sections facing each other across a narrow acting platform that divided the room in half along its short axis. From the end of the room opposite the balcony, a wooden walkway supported by metal posts curved up over the central platform and the two audience sections and then sloped down again to where it had started, making a generally circular "road" in space. Actors not only performed on the central stage and the "skyway" but in the rear of the spectator groups and among them. To emphasize scenically this interpenetration of audience and performance, real fruit trees were placed throughout the hall and flowering branches hung from overhead.

A more austere example of Okhlopkov's spatial concerns was his production of *Mother* by Maxim Gorky. A basic arena arrangement was used with a low, round, stepped acting platform rising from a central square surrounded by raked seats. But aisles at each corner of the square connected with peripheral acting space behind the audience, along the walls of the room. (It was somewhat like the stage Apollinaire had despaired of getting two decades earlier.) Okhlopkov designed the space, in the words of Norris Houghton in *Moscow Rehearsals,* "to bring about the meeting of actor and audience so that it will be impossible to separate the two—to surround the audience with actors just as the actors are surrounded by audience."

Although some credit Okhlopkov with eliminating the stage and blending the stage and auditorium together, it would seem that he actually "fragmented" *the* stage, dividing it into many small stages placed behind, around, and above the audience as well as in front of it. Apparently in only one production did Okhlopkov do away with the platform that indicates "this is acting area" (although he did not do away with the seats that indicate "this is audience area"). For *The Iron Flood* by Serafimovich, an arching "sky" of blue canvas concealed the walls and ceiling of the Realistic Theatre; rocks, trees, and bushes turned the floor into a hillside. It was as if the audience was on stage and a realistic fourth wall had been dropped behind them: The entire hall was filled with the "setting." The scene was the encampment of a unit of the Red army during the civil war, and action took place in all parts of the space. Not only were the spectators "in" the action, but all the senses were forcefully involved: In *Moscow Theatres* Victor Komissarzhevsky explains that "It seemed that the smells of steppe wormwood, of horses' sweat, and the smoke of fires filled the theatre."

If Antonin Artaud was not able to give tangible shape to his vision, he was one of the most passionate and forceful spokesmen for environmental theatre, and his writings have had a great influence on contemporary thought. In "The Theatre of Cruelty (First Manifesto)," published in *The Theatre and Its Double*, Artaud asks for a "diffusion of action over an immense space." This is to be achieved by remodeling a "hangar or barn" to eliminate any barriers between performers and spectators: The stage and auditorium are to be replaced by "a single site." The spectators would be seated in the middle of the space and action would take place around them, in the four corners of the room, and in the center where diffuse, simultaneous, and distributed action could be concentrated. Galleries around the hall would also carry the performance above the audience, filling the space three-dimensionally.

Hellzapoppin, which opened in New York on September 22, 1938, was really two shows in one: In part it was a revue headed by Olsen and Johnson (who were "responsible" to an unrecorded extent for the whole show) that included the usual singers, dancers, comics, imitators, magicians, and so forth, and in part an aggressive use of the whole auditorium to "involve" the spectator. John Anderson, in his review in *The New York Journal-American,* said the performance did "everything to the audience except drag it up on the stage and spit in its eye." After a prologue, acclaimed by all the critics, in which Hitler, Mussolini, Roosevelt, and John L. Lewis all appeared on film praising Olsen and Johnson and their revue in dubbed voices—Hitler spoke with a Jewish accent and Mussolini in Negro dialect—much of the performance was carried on by "plants" in the house. Barkers walked up and down the aisles selling toy balloons, candy, gum, and souvenirs; one speculator hawked tickets to the then popular *I Married An Angel.* There were several "running gags": A florist repeatedly attempted to deliver a small plant to "Mrs. Jones," and by the end of the performance it had grown into a large tree he could no longer carry; the audience was told that "The Phantom" would escape from a strait jacket in five seconds, but he did not and spent the rest of the evening struggling on and off the stage; a woman loudly searched for "Oscar," and when, late in the performance, she was invited onto the stage and "killed" (blank pistols were numerous and were frequently used), a man began calling for "Lena." An almost nude man appeared in an upper balcony on a horse; an orangutan watched the show from another box; a man in a gorilla costume dragged a screaming girl out of a stage box and carried her off. The lights went out and puffed rice was scattered over the spectators while a voice on the loudspeaker explained that it was "only bushels and bushels of spiders." At other times, eggs, bananas, and clothing were thrown into the audience. Even at intermission, a clown bothered the spectators. One element of Olsen and Johnson's routine carried audience involvement to a point where it would have great pertinence to some spectators while being completely pointless to others: They went to the trouble of finding out the names of notable people in attendance at the performance and incorporated them into their act.

As Okhlopkov did in the 1930's, Jerzy Grotowski works in a rather small, rectangular, flat-floored theatre, and he establishes a different audience-performance relationship for each play. His presentations at the Theatre Laboratory in Opole, Poland, show that this relationship can be as creatively expressive of the conceptual core as any other element in the production. His fragmentation of *the* stage into a multiplicity of environmental acting areas reached the point in his version of Adam Mickiewicz' *The Ancestors* that individual spectators were spatially isolated, facing in different directions, and the action took place among them: Performance and audience interpermeated, both filling the entire hall.

Richard Schechner has studied with Grotowski, and he uses Grotowski methods, in part, when working with his Performance Group. *Dionysus in 69* was developed and staged by Schechner in a New York garage rather than in a traditional theatre in order to make maximum use of environmental possibilities. Although much of the action occurred in a central playing space, there were no chairs to distinguish performance area from acting area. For the most part, the spectators sat or stood on carpet-covered levels, platforms, and towers that were also used, at times, by the actors.

Earlier in this essay, I indicated that the word "environment" had two slightly different meanings, and I related examples of environmental theatre to that definition which is most pure, theoretical, and abstract. But if the word "environment" indicates the space that surrounds a person and anything that occupies that space, it may also be thought of, in a less theoretical and more concrete way, as "the particular world in which we live" or, as Webster's dictionary says, "the aggregate of all the external conditions and influences affecting the life and development of a human being." Using this sense of the word in the phrase "environmental theatre," we have a theatre that rejects theatre buildings as "artificial" and that uses the real places and "theatrical equipment" of everyday life.

Of course merely because a play is performed on the street or in the countryside rather than in a theatre does not make it environmental. A theatre is as physically "real" as any other arrangement of spatial limitation. But just as it has been suggested that the physical elements that surround the spectator must somehow become an intrinsic part of the performance before we can consider that performance environmental, so only the performance in "the everyday world" that makes intrinsic use of the materials of that world can be thought of as environmental theatre.

As Allardyce Nicoll points out, *Iphigenia at Aulis* makes particular early reference to Sirius and, somewhat later, to dawn. Original performances of the play actually started at sunrise when Greek audiences could still see the Dog Star; although the script is not environmental, these early performances certainly were, at least in these two "appropriations" of elements from the natural surroundings.

In 1920 Max Reinhardt staged Hugo von Hofmannsthal's

version of *Everyman* in the Domplatz, or square, in front of the great cathedral in Salzburg. As people watched from the streets and from the windows of houses along the square, the whole city, including the medieval castle that rises on a wooded mountain in the center of Salzburg, became part of the performance. It was still daylight when the actors entered from the neighboring squares, but after the sun went down torches moved through the landscape. Von Hofmannsthal has described how "cries uttered by invisible spirits to warn Everyman of his approaching death [were heard] from the church [in front of which the stage had been built] and all the church towers of the city as twilight deepened about the 5000 spectators."

Not unlike the restaging in this country of battles from the Revolution or the Civil War using authentic weapons and uniforms, the Russians reenacted their seizure of the Winter Palace on the actual site in Petrograd. Apparently such dramatic re-creations took place on the first three anniversaries of the October, 1917, event. There is some confusion because different sources apply different dates to the same photograph. Perhaps this should not be surprising: At least one photograph of a reenactment of *The Storming of the Winter Palace* has been reproduced in histories of the Revolution as representing the actual event. Although the photograph of an infantry charge toward the palace looks quite realistic, the performance itself was inaccurate for two reasons: It intentionally included many obviously theatrical elements performed on two stages joined by a bridge, and historians now seem to be of the opinion that the Reds did not actually "storm" the palace at all but got in through a poorly guarded back door. At any rate, the actual site of the overthrow of Alexander Kerensky's Provisional Government was used for at least two or three mass spectacles that involved thousands of performers—1000 citizens and a fully equipped battalion of infantry in the 1918 performance supervised and designed by Nathan Altman; 8000 "actors" and 500 musicians in the 1920 spectacle staged by Evreinov—and mixed symbolic and decorative aspects with an attempt at a historical naturalism. On the first anniversary in

1918, fifty actors all played Kerensky with identical simultaneous movements because a single human figure would have
been lost in the large square in front of the palace. The cruiser
Aurora, lying in the nearby Neva River, added her gunfire to
that of the rifles and machine guns firing at the palace just as
she had done the year before. Her ammunition, of course, was
identical with that which some authorities say was used in
1917: blanks.

In 1924 Sergei Eisenstein staged a play, *Gas Works*, on the
various steel walkways and ladders of the Moscow Gas Works.
But the use of a "found" environment is not limited to plays.
Many logical performances have made use of the unique characteristics of a particular place: Allan Kaprow presented *Courtyard* in the tall, roofed, central court of an old hotel in New
York; Claes Oldenburg did *Autobodys* in a California parking
lot; Dick Higgins' *The Tart* took place in a Queens boxing
arena, and Oldenburg's *Washes* in a swimming pool.

The mere fact that a stage is outdoors does not mean that
performances on it are necessarily environmental. The Open
Air Theatre in Tampere, Finland, makes particular use, however, of the potentialities of the surrounding landscape in at
least one production. This presentation of a war play involves
a camouflaged machine gun nest in the nearby forest, trucks
moving about, and even an airplane that plays its part "on
cue."

(The Open Air Theatre, which seats 800 people, is an interesting variation on the annular stage. The central seating section is motorized so that the audience may be turned to face
any portion of the peripheral playing area. It seems that in the
existing examples of this type of staging, the audience is quite
steeply raked, channeling perception toward the front. The
relationship of the audience to the annular stage—ignoring, for
the moment, such environmental embellishments as a plane
flying overhead—is essentially frontal, and rotation of the audience seems to be only another way of changing scenery. But
the spectator moves, and this movement can easily be made an
intrinsic part of the performance, suggesting that all movement

of the spectator through space can be considered as yet another dimension of environmental theatre. The spectator might be free to move about, as he was in the 360-degree film presentation at the New York State pavilion or at Whitman's *The Night Time Sky*, for example. Or he might become part of a procession, as it were, asked to proceed through one section of the performance to another, as in Oldenburg's Dallas *Injun*. Or his movement might be achieved mechanically as in the various "rides" at the New York World's Fair in which spectators seated in moving conveyances of various kinds looked at displays as they moved past.)

In terms of our broadest definition of "environment," the *Instantaneous Invasion* section of Marta Minujin's *Simultaneity in Simultaneity* could be considered a unique type of environmental theatre. Elements of the presentation were carried simultaneously by two television stations and a radio station in Buenos Aires, Argentina. Each spectator experienced the performance while alone in his own home, switching television channels when directed in order to follow the piece. During the ten minutes that the program lasted, 500 people in a special audience received a telephone call and 100 of them received telegrams. Minujin was using various mass media to create a kind of private environmental theatre.

——————————— AUDIENCE PARTICIPATION

One evening when I was waiting in the usual crowd to pick up a reservation for a program at Judson Memorial Church, a stranger said, "I know you!" "Maybe you know my brother," I answered, being quite familiar with that form of mistaken identity. He thought for a moment. "I know! You're a dancer! You danced for Yvonne Rainer." I was quite flattered and acknowledged that he was correct. Actually, I am not a trained dancer. But I did walk around for Yvonne in one of her dances.

Her contribution to the 9 *Evenings: Theatre and Engineering* program at the Twenty-fifth Street Armory was a piece called *Carriage Discreteness.* A large rectangle about the size of a basketball court was divided into consecutively numbered squares, and on it were placed various white rectangular solids of different kinds—mattresses, mattress-sized wooden boxes, foam blocks, rubber sheets, wooden beams, and so forth. Each of the ten "dancers," of whom I was one, wore walkie-talkie radios and followed the directions that were broadcast to him. Only one person, or at most, two people, moved at one time, walking to the object he was directed to move, picking it up, carrying it to the designated square, and setting it down. Certain peripheral images were added, but the focus of the long piece was this sequence of simple movements.

After the first performance I was told that a girl had come out of the audience, played with a few of the small blocks for awhile, and then gone back to her seat. I had not seen her. When we finished the task that Yvonne assigned over the radio, we could stand or sit in whatever position we wished, but we were supposed to remain motionless, and I had apparently been facing the other way. It was probably because of the story, however, that I was somewhat prepared when, during the second performance of the piece, a man walked out of the audience, picked up one of the small foam blocks, and tossed it at Julie Judd, who stood near me. As I "politely but firmly" led him out, he looked up appealingly at the spectators (almost tripping on the retaining rope), and feebly said, "I was just trying to liven things up." Bob Ashley, of the ONCE group in Michigan, was convinced that since the interruptions occurred at about the same time in both performances they were planned parts of the piece.

Although I could ponder about how all it takes to be a hero is to be in the right place at the right time, the element of spectator involvement during Yvonne's piece that had the most effect on me happened on the first evening. Because of its basically uninflected structure, the performance was boring for many people. And they knew that we were getting our directions over the walkie-talkie radios. Spectators began to shout, clap, and stamp on the wooden bleachers. Static caused by the steel girders of the armory made radio reception difficult, and the noise now made it practically impossible to hear. Soon, it seemed that all 1500 people in the audience were venting their anger at us. Just at that moment, Yvonne directed me to carry one of the blocks to square number one, the closest point to the audience. As I set it down, I had the impulse to turn my back, but that seemed like a cowardly thing to do. I folded my arms and stared at the clamorous packed stands, at least trying to indicate that I believed in Yvonne and what she was trying to do. They were exceedingly uncomfortable moments for all of us. At last the noise subsided, but one could not help but feel that simplistic notions of "audience participation" were being promulgated far too widely.

The Activity:
A New
Art Form

No art form has strictly defined limits. At what point, for example, does prose become poetry? Passages from novels have been included in anthologies of poetry. It seems that Irish novelists and playwrights are considered "poetic" if they merely capture the rhythms and colorful imagery of their everyday speech. At the other extreme, the abstract poetry of Hugo Ball, Raoul Hausmann, and Kurt Schwitters, among others, moves toward music in its use of sound without meaning; Schwitters' *Ursonata* actually was written in sonata form. Many essentially two-dimensional canvases abjure the traditional rectangular format; other shaped canvases protrude to varying degrees into the space of the room. Countless examples of this kind of art—works that extend the definition of an art form to its limits or combine the characteristics of two or more forms—could be given. Taken as a whole, they represent one of the dominant trends in avant-garde art.

This does not mean, however, that the traditional definitions of the various art forms are no longer useful or significant. Definitions properly exist as norms rather than as absolute restrictions. This is the way they function in everyday speech. If I say "painting" or "sculpture" or "performance," you know what I mean. The terms act as a measure of central tendency rather than as strict and pedantic limitations. It is pointless, therefore, to invent a new term unless a work does not, *in general*, fit in an existing category. The traditional words will suffice. There is no need, for example, to claim that "mixed media" performances are a new art form when, since they are done for an audience, they can easily be seen as a kind of theatre. (Actually we can frequently be even more exact in this case: Drama, dance, and opera—all forms of theatre—make use of mixed media.) Useful adjectives should not be confused with the nouns naming forms of art. This does not mean that new terms cannot be coined, but new terminology is not needed unless it increases the precision of communication and actually indicates a significant difference from traditionally defined forms.

We have all heard so many fanciful, extravagant, and un-founded claims of "new" developments in art that we tend to dismiss such statements as immature and intellectually un-rewarding. It is obvious that new names are sometimes coined merely in an attempt to attract attention and to indicate or create originality where none exists. When we view designa-tions as referring to central tendency, it is even possible to believe that, theoretically, no new art form could exist: Styles, modes, manners, and materials of art may change, the reason-ing would run, but there can be no new form such as music, sculpture, or theatre, which already include every sensory possibility.

It is with all seriousness, then, and, I believe, with awareness of the implications, that I suggest that an entirely new form of art has recently been developed. I propose that the distinguishing characteristics of this form are basically so completely different from all traditional categories as to require a special name and that the nature and implications of this new form are of theoretical and practical importance.

There is a subjective aspect to all art. Art exists, at least in part, in our personal experience of the work. But in all traditional art, the work—the thing that gives the art its objective reality—is available to everyone. Experiences of a work may differ, and spectators at a performance necessarily view it from different distances and angles, for example, but the thing is there to be perceived. In the new art form under discussion, the "thing" has moved inside the body, so to speak. The actions of the person himself become the object of his own attention. This work of art can only be seen by one person, and it can only be viewed from within. Since the object of the aesthetic experience has become the self-perceived behavior of an individual, I refer to the form as "Activities": One performs "an Activity." (As with the form of theatre called "Happenings," I use an initial capital. Any happening is not a Happening, nor any activity an Activity.)

The origins of the Activity can be traced at least as far back as postwar Dada. One of Max Ernst's contributions to the infamous 1920 Dada exhibition in Cologne was a wooden object to which a hatchet was attached by a chain: It seemed a demand or challenge to substitute the activity of destroying the work for aesthetic contemplation. In "The Dada Spirit in Painting," included in *The Dada Painters and Poets* edited by Robert Motherwell, Georges Hugnet tells us of Jean (Hans) Arp's *Egg Board* "with directions for use." The "board" was apparently one of Arp's many wooden reliefs, and the instructions for its use consisted of five "movements":

1. chop several eggs
2. split some wood
3. ring the bells

4. masturbate

5. throw the egg in the navel

This may have been Arp's 1922 *Egg Board*, a painted relief of several identical human silhouettes, each with a large raised egg-shaped navel. The description implies a single, indented navel, however, and the nature of the bells remains a mystery. At any rate, that particular *Egg Board* served, in Arp's words, as the "coat of arms" for a "game for the upper ten thousand, in which the participants leave the arena covered with egg yolk from top to toe." In this game intended to enlighten the bourgeoisie, the players were visualized "smashing eggs with the eggboard through the goal . . . the use of hardboiled eggs is unfair."

The black humor of the Dadaists and their attempt to de-sanctify art by using everyday materials were congenial to Activities, and several contemporary examples of Activities can be found in the "newspapers" or broadsides published by Fluxus, a semiformal neo-Dada group of artists. Ben Vautier, for example, authored *Fifty-eight Propositions for One Page* (1965) in which he gave fifty-seven directions (one of the boxes is blank) for things to do with the page: "hide this," "touch with one finger the whole surface of the page," and so forth. His direction "hang this page on a string—don't touch it—wait till it disappears" is reminiscent: When Marcel Duchamp was in Buenos Aires in 1918, he wrote to his sister Suzanne in Paris, directing her to hang a geometry textbook on the balcony of her apartment.

Duchamp's creation can be said to have three aspects: the performance of the activity (hanging the book), the ready-made that was created (the hanging book), and the knowledge of the whole (available to Duchamp even at a distance). If the emphasis is on the first of these, the work could be considered an Activity. Thus it is important to distinguish between *external* sensory experiences such as seeing and hearing and *internal* experiences such as proprioception, kinesthesia, and thought. If we do not regard Arp's *Egg Board* as merely a joke, as I do not, we can see that the actions could theoretically be done for an audience as a performance; Duchamp's geometry book became, in one sense, a piece of sculpture that could be looked at. But, at least in Arp's case, the emphasis seems to be on the subjective experience of performing the piece rather than on its external characteristics. It seems to be intended to be performed in private for the sole aesthetic benefit of the performer. If a work of art is intended for the introspective attention of the performer, it can be called an Activity.

Although Activities do not necessarily involve a sense of play, they could be compared to games that—as seems to be the case with Arp's eggboard game—are played for their own sake rather than for the sake of winning or for enjoyment by an audience. Like scientific experiments and religious ritual, Activities are "performed." Even though the behavior in carrying out an Activity is not necessarily ritualized, both Activity and ritual are performed for the sake of the action itself or for the sake of the thing that is done. Both may be performed in solitude. They may also be done by more than one person, and an audience does not change the orientation of either. An Activity is like a ritual that has no theological or metaphysical efficacy.

In *An Anthology of Chance Operations*, edited and published in 1963 by LaMonte Young and Jackson MacLow, Walter De Maria propounded a theory of "meaningless work." He was discussing his approach to what I have chosen to call "Activities." Explaining what kinds of work are meaningless, he said "caution should be taken that the work chosen should not be too pleasurable, lest pleasure becomes the purpose of the work." He described his *Meaningless Work Boxes* (1960) in which various things are moved from one box to another. He gave the procedure for his *Beach Crawl*, involving the systematic placement and replacement of three stones: It ends with the direction, "Then shout as loud as you can 'Well that's new isn't it?' Then throw the three stones into the ocean." De Maria also wrote about his *Art Yard* (1960), "sort of a big hole in the ground" where "digging the hole would be part of the art." In the proposed *Art Yard* there were to be stands for formally dressed spectators, but people would also be allowed to participate. This was somewhat in contradiction to his stated principle that "to be fully understood, meaningless work should be done alone or else it becomes entertainment for others."

It is important to emphasize that Activities are not a form of theatre. Theatre requires and demands an audience. Activities do not. Of course, any action or behavior could have an accidental audience. This, in itself, would not create theatre. It is only when a performance is intentionally done *for* an audience that theatre exists. *Mirror* by Chieko Shiomi, for example, instructs the performer to stand on a sandy beach facing away from the sea; while looking into a mirror, he is to walk backward into the water. Spectators are not considered in the piece. Although they obviously could be present, it was not composed to be watched but to be done.

It is the performance aspect of Activities that relates them theoretically to theatre even though they are a different form. There is a saying among theatre people, that "There are no small parts, only small actors." Hypothetically considering role-playing as an Activity rather than as an object for appreciation by an audience, this becomes untrue. Acting the part of Hamlet is entirely different from merely reading the play silently to oneself, and the person who acts out the part in the privacy of his own room or in a group reading unattended by spectators is having an experience similar to that of the performer in an Activity. Since only the person performing an Activity may know the quality of the piece, an apparently "bad" actor, as judged by an observer, may be creating an important experience for himself. (One wonders to what extent actors may be introspectively involved with this kind of perception rather than with the creation of an objective character for consideration by an audience.)

If Activities can, in certain situations, be erroneously viewed as theatre, they may also tend toward sculpture. *Recipe* by

George Brecht gives directions for arranging a piece of paper on a piece of cloth, marking the paper with a burnt match, arranging two pieces of string and a glass on the cloth, and placing an egg in the glass. The finished construction can be viewed as a piece of sculpture or an assemblage, and Brecht does not indicate whether or not this is the most important element. If only because of the impermanence of the "ingredients" in *Recipe* and the fact that they are not fastened together, the piece seems more involved with the act of construction than with the finished product.

Brecht is one of the foremost exponents of this type of work, although it is often ambiguous whether the intent is to create theatre, sculpture, or Activity. At times, such as when he directs us to water the telephone when it rings, he shows the bitter humor and involvement with everyday life characteristic of Dada. His pieces tend to be intimate and uncomplicated. One, for example, is a card with a photograph of a child lying on its side with one leg raised in the air, and precise drawings of a thermometer and the reversed face of a clock. As such it could be understood as a kind of printed collage. But directions on the card tell us to place one fingertip on the child's right foot, another fingertip on the bulb of the thermometer, and a small object of any kind on the clock face. Like Arp's *Egg Board*, it is, in a sense, a picture with which the spectator actively collaborates.

Since there are no audience requirements, the performance of an Activity does not need to take place all at once. It may be discontinuous and scattered through time, so to speak. In *Chair* (1963), Robert Ashley gives directions involving a chair that cover a six-day period. On the first day, the chair is decorated as beautifully as possible. On the second day it is broken into small pieces and put into a small cardboard box. Finally, on the sixth day, after other transformations, ashes of the chair, sealed in a beautifully decorated jar, are placed "approximately in the center of a larger jar completely filled with sand." On the seventh day, the performer rests. It is quite clear that the experience of actually going through this procedure would be basically different from that involved in experiencing any other art form.

Thus an Activity may be diffused through space as well as time. Wolf Vostell issued his own ration stamps with elaborate directions about which grocery store to go to on each day and what to buy there. The stores, as I remember, were scattered throughout the whole New York metropolitan area. When buying the designated food, the stamps were, of course, to be presented to the grocer—who had not been informed about the Activity.

Activities such as the ones I have mentioned usually involve a single performer. Allan Kaprow's pieces are conceived for larger numbers. They are a development of his earlier Happenings, and he still refers to them as "Happenings," but they are, so to speak, theatrical performances from which the audience has been removed. This transformation is significant and, as I see it, crucial. Kaprow is virtually alone in working in Activities on this scale, and his work deserves discussion in some detail.

As is quite clear from Kaprow's work, audience participation should not be confused with the performance of an Activity. His earlier Happenings were, indeed, theatre pieces in which audience participation of various kinds was usually involved. At one point in the eponymous *18 Happenings in 6 Parts,* for example, two men who were ostensibly members of the audience left their seats to paint on opposite sides of a canvas panel. This could be called "pseudo-participation" or "figurative participation." The audience is led to believe that certain of its members are taking part in the performance or such participation is symbolized. Of course, "plants," such as the "spectator" who calls out "That's the way it really is!" as part of *The Connection* by Jack Gelber, have also been used in drama. In Kaprow's case, the names of the painters appeared on the "Cast of Participants," but even at that early date he had the inclination or impulse, as yet unrealized, to involve the spectators physically in the creation of the piece:

They, too, were included on the "Cast of Participants," and the final entry read, "The visitors—who sit in various chairs."

A similar form of audience participation could be called "token" or "selected" involvement. In Kaprow's *Courtyard,* for example, some of the standing spectators were offered brooms and asked to sweep. Only a few members of the audience were actually involved, but, as in figurative participation, the whole audience was symbolically taking part in the piece. Both token and figurative participation seem to depend on the belief that a spectator may empathize more easily and completely with another spectator than he could with a performer, creating a psychic involvement with the presentation.

Another type of audience participation is that in which the entire audience takes part in the piece for a certain amount of time. In Kaprow's *A Service for the Dead, 1,* for example, the waiting spectators became part of a parade or procession to get to the place where the main portion of the piece was performed; in his *A Spring Happening,* the spectators were all forced to move out of the way of a power lawnmower.

In all such cases, there is a clearly defined difference between spectators and performers. Certain elements of the performance are not created by the spectators and are directed at, or done for the sake of, the audience. Although the spectator is asked, forced, or allowed to do certain things at certain times, he is basically a passive observer.

Kaprow's latest pieces do not intentionally involve an audience. Spectators are often a possibility or even, in some cases, a likelihood, but the works are not done for them. The first such non-spectator piece that Kaprow attempted was part of a Yam Festival program at George Segal's farm in 1963. Although it was not designed to have an audience, most of the huge crowd on hand that day declined to take part in *Tree* and established a more or less traditional audience-performance relationship by remaining spectators.

Kaprow solved this technical problem in later performances by using only people who had read a description of what was to be done and who had agreed to participate. Although a person might be temporarily inactive, each had a job to do, and there was no audience as such. Kaprow's *Calling* is an example of this kind of piece. The following description appeared in the *Tulane Drama Review*.

Although there were two preliminary meetings at which the people involved received instructions and worked out procedural details, the piece titled *Calling* by Allan Kaprow "officially" began at 4 P.M. on Saturday, August 21, 1965. At that time, on three different street corners in New York, a participant was waiting: a girl stood on the southwest corner of Fifth Avenue and Fourteenth Street, another girl was on the northeast corner of Hudson and Christopher Streets, and a man waited at Tenth Avenue and Forty-second Street. Each carried a paper bag which contained aluminum foil, muslin, and a ball of cord.

The people had been waiting for at least half an hour, when, at 4:30 P.M., cars stopped near each of them, and their names were called. They got into the cars. As they were driven randomly about the city (the schedule allowed ample time before they had to be at the next required locations), the three people were completely covered with aluminum foil.

At 4:50 P.M., each car parked, all occupants except the foil-wrapped figure got out, the car was locked and a coin placed in the meter. During their rides the foil-covered participants had occasionally caused mild surprise and curiosity (as they would continue to do), and the interest of passersby was somewhat greater now that the cars were parked. The girl who had waited at Fifth Avenue and Fourteenth Street was now in the parking area above Union Square at Eighteenth Street and Park Avenue South; the second girl had been taken from Hudson and Christopher Streets to the north side of Fourteenth Street between Fifth and Sixth Avenues; and the man picked up at Tenth Avenue and Forty-second Street was sitting in a parked car on the south side of Twenty-third Street between Eighth and Ninth Avenues.

Other participants were waiting at these points. While the first three cars had been making their pickups, these second groups had parked three more cars at various public parking garages. (The six cars were of different makes and models, ranging from a large station wagon to a small Volkswagen. The public nature of the garages used was important because the people could park their own cars rather than having an attendant do it.) Now the driver of each of the first three cars traded keys with the driver in the waiting group, received a parking stub, and was informed of the exact location (by floor, aisle, row, etc.) in which the "second stage" cars had been parked. The group from each of the first three cars proceeded by taxi or subway to the parking garages, leaving their silver "packages" in the locked cars.

The "second stage" crews drove off with the wrapped people. Their destination was the same parking garage at which they had each left a "second stage" car less than an hour earlier, but there was no need to hurry, and as the cars drove about the silver wrappings of their special passengers were removed and the people were rewrapped in muslin and tied with cord.

At 5:20 P.M., the "first stage" cars with their new drivers and crews arrived at the parking garages. The girl who had started at Fifth Avenue and Fourteenth Street was now at the Municipal Parking Garage on Eighth Avenue between Fifty-third and Fifty-fourth Streets; the second girl was taken to the Coliseum Parking Garage at Fifty-ninth Street and Broadway; and the man was driven to the Lincoln Center garage on Sixty-fifth Street near Broadway. The wrapped people were taken out of their cars and left on the concrete. The cars drove off. The other participants— who had originally picked up and wrapped the three "packages" and left them in the locked cars—picked up the muslin-wrapped figures and loaded them into the "second stage" cars.

Leaving their respective garages soon after 5:20 P.M., the three cars drove about the city until 5:45 P.M., when they were scheduled to deposit their wrapped passengers at Grand Central Station. Because of the heavy traffic, however, all three cars did not arrive at exactly the same moment, and it was more than five minutes before all three wrapped people were carried into the station and propped against the information booth. When the third "package" arrived, a large crowd had already gathered, and the other two participants had begun calling out each other's names. For some time each of the three people called out the names of the other two. Then they removed their wrappings and went directly to telephone booths.

Each of the three dialed the number of one of the participants who had helped to wrap or drive them during the second stage. (The "second stage" people had dispersed and gone home after leaving the parking garages, as the others had done immediately after leaving the wrapped people at Grand Central.) For five minutes the three people in Grand Central and the people in the three apartments throughout the city listened to the ringing. After each telephone had rung fifty times, it was picked up. "Hello." The correct name was quizzically asked, but the recipient hung up without saying anything more. Saturday's part of *Calling* was complete.

The next day—a Sunday of overcast skies and very light scattered rain—the participants all met at a farm in New Jersey. Because of trouble with one of the cars, some of them were delayed on the one-hour drive, and the second part of the piece did not begin until late afternoon.

After receiving brief instructions, all of the people except the three who had been wrapped in foil and muslin on the preceding day filed into a wooded area to the rear of the farm house. No paths were visible among the trees. The ground was soft and wet, and water fell from the foliage when it was pushed out of the way. Four or five of the people were asked to wait at each of five previously selected locations until all had been assigned a spot. At each of the locations a piece of heavy sailcloth with a hole in the center dangled from ropes attached to the branch of a tree, and Kaprow demonstrated how, when the signal was given, the volunteer in each group was to climb into the canvas sling and hang head downward.

Each group was isolated in the damp woods. None of the people in one group could see any of the participants in any of the other groups. It was quiet. After a time Kaprow's voice was heard calling "Come on" to the two girls and the man who had been left behind when the others entered the woods. At each location one person climbed into the apparatus and hung upside-down. His head, thrust through the hole in the sailcloth, was perhaps a foot above the ground, and the arms and legs were supported by ropes on either side.

When the three "searchers" reached the edge of the woods, they called out the names of the five people—the three men and two women—who, somewhere out of their sight, were hanging inverted among the trees. When a hanging person's name was called, he and the three or four participants who were sitting or squatting silently nearby answered, "Here." By following the sounds, the trio located each hanging person and quickly cut and ripped away all his or her clothing before moving on to find the next group. The calling and responses continued until the last hanging person was found and stripped of clothing. Again the woods were silent.

The people in the first group, when they became aware of the final departure of the three searchers, began to call out the names of the four people who hung at the other locations. The others began to call, too. For perhaps ten minutes the names of the five hanging people were the material for a random vocal symphony sounding from various locations and with various volumes and qualities. Finally the pauses in the calling grew longer, and the voices stopped. The five people who had been stripped of their clothing still hung in their uncomfortable positions. After a moment, a sound was heard among the trees indicating that someone had begun to leave. The hanging people swung down, and everyone moved slowly and quietly out of the woods.

If we compare *Calling* to drama, it was as if the scenes of a play were done not only at different places, but at different places at the same time. *No one,* including Kaprow himself, saw all of the actions of which the piece was composed. But each of the participants did experience the piece in its entirety. They were not only aware of their own actions and those of the other participants with whom they were directly involved, but they each had read the script and had been briefed. They knew what was taking place in other parts of the city even though they could not be there, and this knowledge became part of the aesthetic experience. Although *Calling* intentionally moved from the private to the public—what could be more public than the information booth at Grand Central?—it existed in its totality only in the experience of each individual performer.

(On the other hand, it is doubtful whether many of the accidental spectators of the various elements of *Calling* ever learned exactly what it was they had seen. When, during their travels through the city, the participants were forced to explain themselves, they sometimes said that they were doing advance location work on a children's film about people who were mistakenly wrapped as packages and sent around the world.)

Since Activities do not take place in any special place, such as a theatre, and employ everyday behavior, such as making telephone calls or driving a car, there is the potential for "blurring" the "edges" of the work, so to speak, and making the observer or participant wonder about or question its limits. When I participated in *Calling*, several of us went to a soda fountain after Kaprow's briefing session to pass the time until we were scheduled to begin our part of the performance. Perhaps because of the sense of anticipation, the conspiratorial qualities of the particular piece, or the feeling of adventure that was generated, it was as if everything that we said and did was already part of the piece. This particular experience was, of course, not a unique case of the psychological imposition of an art attitude on everyday life. It is similar to the moments when the stains on the walls of the subway tunnel are seen as abstract expressionist paintings or when the supplies in the kitchen all take on the character of Pop Art. It was no less striking or forceful than the time I suddenly and unexpectedly *saw* the forest, without any intentional "translation" on my part, exactly the way Cézanne would have painted it. But Activities, by their basic nature, can exploit the possibility of fusion with everyday life more directly and easily than any other art form. This illustrates the important point that the aesthetic experience involved is basically cerebral rather than perceptual.

In most performances of any kind, the physical, and therefore the mental, limits of the piece are established quite clearly by directions, physical cues, or conventions. An Activity, for example, does not begin with the preliminary preparations such as gathering required materials any more than the rehearsal of a play is the play itself. In both cases, the distinction is not in the observable character of the actions but in the mental state of the observer as qualified by information. Even so, it may be somewhat ambiguous, as I have shown, exactly where an Activity begins or ends. (This is not, however, unique to the form. Long before *The Connection* and Peter Brook's version of *Marat/Sade*, spectators entered theatres to find the curtain up and performers already doing things on stage. Certain productions of plays also attempt to eliminate clear-cut beginnings and endings.)

The spatial and temporal disjunction of *Calling* was manifested even more strongly in Kaprow's *Self-Service*. It was performed in Boston, New York, and Los Angeles from June through September, 1967; the participants in the various cities selected activities from the list Kaprow provided and were free to perform them at any time during the four-month period. One of the instructions is interesting because it illustrates that an Activity may have no external manifestations that could indicate to a passerby that a work is being performed. It read: *People stand on bridges, on street corners, watch cars pass. After two hundred red ones, they leave.*

All of Kaprow's most recent Activities demonstrate a common character that could be called "sculptural." They are not, of course, actually sculpture, nor do they involve the creation of sculpture. The performances usually do not leave a physical product behind. But they do involve the creation of things. The performance aspect of the work consists of the fabrication of very large constructions of various kinds scaled to the landscape. These "sculptural" constructions give the piece its structure and character.

The first of these pieces was *Fluids*, performed in Los Angeles in November, 1967. Identical structures made of blocks of ice were built during a three-day period at fifteen different places around the metropolitan area: with closed walls following a rectangular plan, the roofless boxes—each thirty feet long, ten feet wide, and eight feet high—appeared solid when seen from ground level. *Fluids* consisted of the erection of the fifteen structures, each of which was made up of 648 fifty-pound blocks of ice and took about three-and-a-half hours to build. The melting of the ice, which took about twelve hours for each unit, was not considered part of the piece.

Runner, created by Kaprow in a suburb of St. Louis in February, 1968, also involved the appearance and disappearance of a physical structure. In this case, tar paper was unrolled along the shoulder of a gently curving concrete road and weighted with concrete blocks every twenty feet for a distance of one mile. On the following day, two more layers of tar paper and blocks were added, beginning each time from the end where the preceding layer had terminated. Kaprow explains that he was making "a road beside a road" and that the title, *Runner,* "referred to a carpet or hallway runner, as well as to someone running (along a road)." The tar paper and bricks were removed on the third day.

To Kaprow, of course, it was the work involved, which could be seen as a parody and imitation of actual road construction, that really made up the piece: ". . . the sweat and cold were *real* ingredients." In this, his recent pieces resemble the "meaningless work" of Walter De Maria. The work on *Runner* was complicated by a man and his son who deliberately ripped up the tar paper. Finally the police were called to protect the project, the scattered pieces of tar paper were picked up, and *Runner* was completed. The unforeseen events became part of the piece.

Since Kaprow first attempted to eliminate the audience at his performances, he has been bothered by the concurrent necessity of eliminating photographers. He wanted photographs of his work as a record and for publicity, but a photographer was, in theory and in actuality, a spectator. In *Transfer,* performed one week after *Runner* in Middletown, Connecticut, he succeeded in the complete integration of the photographer into the piece. A systemic work, *Transfer* consisted of transporting 100 metal barrels from one site to another. At each site the barrels were unloaded from the two rented trucks, stacked in an orderly fashion, sprayed a single uniform color, and put back into the trucks for "transfer" to another location. Including the chemical plant where the unpainted drums were picked up to begin the sequence, there were nine sites. The manner of stacking at each site was different and usually had some reference to a prominent feature of the environment: A ski slope in one location suggested a ski slope shape for the pile of drums, the town hall was imitated, and so forth. At each of the nine sites, Kaprow had the participants pose for what his directions called a "triumphal photograph." The actions of picture taking were made an intrinsic structural element in the Activity.

Whether an Activity involves many participants, as in Kaprow's work, or a single performer, as in George Brecht's pieces, the fundamental principle is the same. Some Activities relate more to one art form than to another, and there is no art form to which they could not relate, but these are questions of style rather than form. The important thing is the basic characteristic of interiorization that makes the Activity entirely different from any other art. Their development at this time in history seems to be another indication of man's concern with the dimensions of his own consciousness. It can also be seen as a refusal on the part of artists to place limits upon the areas and materials of their work. And, perhaps most important of all, Activities demonstrate in a very direct way the fact that all art essentially exists as personal experience.

DESTRUCTION IN ART, I

For the Destruction in Art evening at the Judson Memorial Church in March, 1968, the enclosed rear yard of the church was arranged like a miniature midway. Each artist had his own display area: Hermann Nitsch was preparing a performance involving the skinned carcass of a lamb, Lil Picard sat wrapped in bandages, Geoff and Bici Hendricks silently offered ice picks to the spectators so that they could hack at a large block of ice. People wandered from one exhibit to another or stood in small groups talking. It was quite crowded and somewhat festive.

I was speaking with Lucy Lippard when she said, "We'd better get out of the way, or we'll get spattered with blood." Not far from us a live black chicken was hanging upside-down at the end of a cord tied to a tree branch. Farther away a white chicken was being hung in the same way, symmetrically balancing the first. We knew that Ralph Ortiz was scheduled to perform a piece called, as I remember, *The Destruction of White Henny and Black Penny.* He had killed chickens in other performances; obviously two were to die that evening. We moved away and continued to talk.

Suddenly John Wilcock was pushing his way through the crowd nearby with the black chicken under his arm, a short length of the severed cord trailing behind from the still-bound claws. He disappeared around a fence into the dark unpaved rear section of the long, narrow yard. No one attempted to follow him. Perhaps Ortiz and the others did not even know the chicken had been taken. Everyone went on talking. Then John was back, moving past me, with a grim look. "Did you free the black chicken?" I asked. He stopped and nodded, folding up a large pocket knife. "How about the white one?"

"It's still there."

"Well, let's go get it."

Turning suddenly, I began dodging quickly through the crowd toward the other end of the yard. I didn't look back but I knew John was right behind me. The white chicken was hanging at about shoulder height, surrounded by chatting people who were paying no attention to it. As I grabbed it, John's knife appeared over my shoulder and cut the cord with one stroke. With mixed feelings of pleasure, excitement, guilt, and determination, I pushed back through the throng and around the fence into the dark rear section of the yard.

No one followed me, not even John. I was nervously untying the cord that had been knotted tightly around the chicken's legs, when Jon Hendricks called from near the fence. "What are you doing?" He was one of the producers of the evening and a friend of mine. "I'm letting him go," I answered, thinking that that was pretty obvious. I wondered briefly about the morality of fighting to save a chicken's life, sure that I would in my aroused state. Jon disappeared without coming any closer. When I tried to push the chicken up and over the rear wall, which was about nine feet high, it kept falling back helplessly flapping its wings. Finally, I dropped it over a low wooden fence at the side. Al Hansen told me later that I had dropped it into the back yard of a discothèque, but everything was dark and there was no music, so he was probably mistaken.

I first met Ira Smolin when we worked together in Allan
Kaprow's *Courtyard,* which was presented in the huge central
roofed courtyard of the Greenwich Hotel on Bleecker Street in
November, 1962. (My description of that piece is included in
my book *Happenings.*) Ira and I were inside a large "volcano"
built of wood and covered with tar paper. We made noise,
threw crumpled balls of tar paper out the top, and so forth.
Ira and his wife, Rose, ran the Smolin Gallery and were interested in avant-garde performances. Over the course of time, I
told them about my background in professional theatre: I had
directed Equity productions in stock and off-Broadway at the
Actors' Playhouse on Sheridan Square, but had given up theatre and turned to sculpture. Earlier in 1962 I had designed

and staged a production of a full-length drama I had written, called *Who Is Cortes?* It was presented by a professional cast for a week to invited audiences in my sculpture studio near Chinatown: a "full house" was about 15 or 20 people. But that had been my only working contact with theatre since I had "retired" and withdrawn from the union. Then Ira Smolin asked me to do something for the Yam Festival that they were sponsoring. I had no idea what I would do, but I said "Yes." We both knew that it would not be a traditional play.

The piece was called *The First and Second Wilderness.* Many of the people who worked on the production have since become quite well-known as artists: Tom Doyle was the Union general and Irwin Fleminger was his lieutenant, Oscar Wineland and John Culjak (the only actor in the piece) were their Confederate counterparts, Sol LeWitt and Jason Crum handled the projections, and Marjorie Strider ran the sound. Marj's sister, Nancy, was the scorekeeper. Letty Eisenhauer and a visiting French girl, who had never seen an American cheerleader, were the cheerleaders. And I was the "referee." The following is a description of the performance as it appeared in the *Tulane Drama Review.*

THE FIRST AND SECOND WILDERNESS

During May, 1963, the Smolin Gallery sponsored a month-long program of Happenings, Events, music, dance, chance theatre, etc., called the Yam Festival ("Yam" is "May" spelled backward). One of the many performances listed on the published calendar was *The First and Second Wilderness,* subtitled *A Civil War Game.* It was presented for one evening only— May 27.

When the spectator climbed four flights of stairs to the loft where the piece was being done, he found himself in a clean, freshly painted room about ninety feet long and twenty feet wide. Near the center of the space, the squares of a large game board had been laid out on the floor with tape. The usual rectangular grid pattern was extended by pyramids of squares at each end which ended in single squares marked "Washington" and "Richmond." Blue and gray cardboard soldiers about two feet tall stood near the opposite ends of the board. Representing infantry and cavalry, the figures were formed of intersecting front and profile silhouettes. Chairs had been placed close to the board at both ends, and leaning against one wall at the side of the game grid was a large spinner. To the right of the spinner, under a sign reading "scoreboard," stood a white ladder. Brightly colored Union and Confederate flags hung on the walls, and behind the rows of chairs, about ten feet from either end of the board, were "horses" built from tables and sawhorses, with wooden saddles and heads made, like huge toys, of stuffed plush. To one side and to the rear of each horse a white sheet hung from the ceiling. Illumination was provided by two bulbs with conical shades that hung over the center of the playing area.

As he entered, each spectator was given two sheets of paper. On one the performers and technicians were listed and the rules of the game were explained, while the other gave the words for several cheers. The rules were very simple: infantry could be moved one space at a time, cavalry could be moved two spaces; not more than five markers could be placed on a square at a time, and all on a square could be moved at once; when opposing markers occupied the same square, the spinner would indicate how many men were "killed" or "taken prisoner"; the side which first moved an infantry marker into the opposing "capital" (the final square) was the winner. (The signs on the spinner were in terms of thousands of men—each marker represented a thousand men. An inner ring on the spinner was to be used if each side had an equal number of markers on a square, while an outer ring was to be read if one side had a numerical advantage.)

Four men in blue and gray uniforms—a Union "General" and "Lieutenant" and Confederates of the same ranks—stood talking to each other and to the spectators. The Confederate Lieutenant placed small bets on the game with members of the audience. When the chairs were filled, people sat along the wall opposite the spinner and stood at both ends of the board.

A tape-recorded bugle call quieted the room. The generals climbed onto the horses on their respective sides, and the lieutenants moved out onto the board. The four men began to recite short statements about the Civil War: that two battles had been fought in Virginia at a place called The Wilderness (the first better known as the battle of Chancellorsville); that the woods caught fire during the first engagement, burning to death many of the wounded on both sides; that General Stonewall Jackson was mistakenly killed by his own men during the second battle, etc. (Each man had been given three statements to say as often and in whatever order he chose. They were directed to think of the mixture of voices as "word jazz," and to try to say each line once when no one else was speaking.) The four voices grew loud and soft, overlapped, were briefly quiet, and spoke out clearly.

Another bugle call was heard on the dual speakers of the sound system (operated by a girl at a table just behind the audience in one corner), and the performers fell silent. A small procession moved onto the board: a girl in a bathing suit held the arm of a tall man dressed entirely in black and wearing sun glasses; they were followed by two girls in cheerleading costume. When they reached the wall where the spinner stood, the girl in the bathing suit climbed the ladder at the right, and the cheerleaders sat on a small bench to the left.

The lieutenants lifted painted flags down from the opposite wall and carried them briskly to the center. The opposing generals walked forward, saluted each other, and shook hands. Nodding to one of the generals to "call" it, the man in black tossed a silver dollar in the air and caught it. The winners and losers of the toss were indicated by the "receiving" and "kicking off" signals performed by football referees, and the performers returned quickly to their places. Civil War songs blared out on the loudspeakers, the mounted generals called orders down to their lieutenants about which markers should be moved, the "referee" placed "mountains" and a "swamp" on the board (making those squares unusable), and the cheerleaders rushed out to lead a cheer. (The cheers were written by Letty Eisenhauer, one of the cheerleaders. Although they had printed copies of the cheers and were frequently quite noisy, the spectators never joined in the formal cheering, preferring merely to watch the acrobatics of the two girls.)

When both "armies" were arranged on the board, the "war" began. The generals shouted orders and comments over the heads of the spectators to their lieutenants, who actually moved the pieces. Their distance from the board hampered the generals' visibility, and the lieutenants tried to keep them informed about enemy movements, offered suggestions, and made comments. (Touches of "characterization" were sometimes used—the terminology of rank, for example, was frequent—but the pervasive impression was one of men in uniform playing a game.)

Soon opposing markers were moved onto the same square, and the man in black whirled the spinner, removed the indicated marker or markers from the board, held them up so that the girl on the ladder could see them clearly, separated the silhouettes, and threw the pieces onto the floor. The scorekeeper in the bathing suit fastened the appropriate number of small blue or gray figures to the wall with transparent tape. The roar of Civil War cannons and rifles and the sound of galloping horses (from a record of a battle recently "refought" with authentic equipment) now alternated with the songs that were coming from the sound system. At times the volume was almost deafening and at other times faded away, according to the taste of the operator. The cheerleaders ran out with paper megaphones to lead a cheer. (They had been told to cheer for "whoever is winning.") "Prisoners" were placed in "stockades" and, at times, exchanges were formally negotiated.

When he felt like it, the man in black blew a police whistle hanging from a cord around his neck, made one of the signals from the visual repertoire of sports officials (he never spoke), and handed a card to one of the lieutenants. Play stopped. The lieutenant read the card out loud, and his words were repeated by each of the other three soldiers.

"Stonewall Jackson is dead," read one of the cards. The performer in black turned out the lights, and the four men in uniform moved slowly together through the spectators and the cardboard markers carrying lighted candles in glass cups. At the center of the board they softly harmonized on one verse of an old song:

> We shall meet, but we shall miss him.
> There will be one vacant chair
> As we gather in the twilight
> To recite our evening prayer.

The man in black touched one of them on the shoulder, and he said, "Let us cross over the river and rest under the shade of the trees." Abruptly, the lights were turned back on, the loudspeakers blared again, and the players returned to their positions.

The other card read, "The Wilderness is on fire." The lights were switched off, and the sound went silent. Lighting a propane torch, the man in black picked up one of the soldiers and began to burn it. Silhouetted by the roaring flame, the heavy fire-resistant cardboard struggled to stay erect. Finally it burned, charred, and crumbled. The man holding it stamped it out on the floor. During the burning, Civil War photographs taken by Matthew Brady—the awkward postures of the dead, soldiers staring blankly at the camera—were thrown from the rear on the hanging sheets at either end by opaque projectors. When the cardboard soldier was finally destroyed, the game resumed. These two interludes were repeated several times in the order and frequency the "referee" felt advisable.

After perhaps twenty or thirty minutes, an infantry marker of one side entered the opposing "capital." The game was over. The man in black walked quickly off. The music surged up. The losing general slowly walked forward to surrender his sword. The cheerleaders rushed out throwing paper flowers and crowned the victors with paper laurel wreaths.

The game was played five times that evening. Some spectators stayed for all of the performances; others came and went.

Perhaps seventy-five people attended. When it was all over, the North had been victorious three times; the South twice.

Unlike a Happening, *The First and Second Wilderness* had an information structure. The various elements related to each other in terms of meaning; they logically explained and justified each other as intellectual symbols and representations. Everything related to and in turn was explained and justified by, the basic image of "(the civil) war is a game." There was nothing abstract or alogical about the way the elements were combined, although no story or plot was involved.

But in December, 1964, I was invited to talk on Happenings at the national convention of the American Educational Theatre Association in Chicago. I felt that it would be almost pointless to speak about something the listeners had not experienced: An example was needed. I worked out what I considered a "pure" example of a Happening. The structure was isomorphic: Each of the consecutive compartments used imagery related to the hand. I made a conscious effort to use as many different production elements or media as I could. Because all of the props had to be transported from New York to Chicago, the performance had to remain relatively simple. As the main performer, I would present as many of the images as I could myself; I tried to keep the number of additional performers at a minimum or to keep their tasks very simple to reduce rehearsal time. The result was *Hand Happening*.

In late June, 1966, I was approached by a producer associated with David Susskind about doing a Happening on television. I met Mr. Susskind, and he was enthusiastic. But they, of course, wanted to see a script. I wrote an expanded version of the *Hand Happening* particularly for television and gave it to them. The only report I got was that when the producer asked Mr. Susskind what he thought of the script, "he shrugged." The following is the television script for *Hand Happening*. (It contains several images that can only be produced on television or on film, and the original staged version included several elements that could not be done with only three performers on television. In the staged version there were "programs" of a single hand print, a "dance" section involving ten or twelve people wearing gloves that glowed in the dark, sounds from throughout the auditorium, and so forth. After I had taken the first bite of the chocolate hand, it was cut in half and passed around to the spectators to be devoured.)

HAND HAPPENING

MAN 1: Seated behind a table, staring at his right hand which is entirely wrapped in a cloth. (Shot is from straight front, as are all other shots unless specified.) Carefully and slowly, he unwraps the hand as it lies on the white table cover. He prods, pokes, and examines it as if it were strange to him.

Behind Man 1 can be seen a wall or row of television sets. Ten seconds after the performance begins, the Happening is kinescoped onto every other tube. Ten seconds after that—twenty seconds after the performance begins—the same initial images appear on the remaining sets. Thus whenever Man 1 performs, the sets behind him can be seen repeating and echoing whatever was seen ten and twenty seconds previously.

MAN 2: Seated behind a table heaped with plaster hands. As camera moves in, the hands stir and shift. Loud steady breathing is heard. The man's real hands, dusted white, appear from beneath the pile of replicas.

GIRL: Stands breathing into a microphone: This is the sound that we have been hearing. On a table near or in front of her, a rubber hand (or hands) rises as it fills with air and then collapses as the air escapes. It continues to expand and contract rhythmically as the camera pulls back (or another cuts in) to show the whole sound stage, all three performers, the cameras, etc. The performers, each at one vertex of an equilateral triangle, face the center. (Perhaps this relationship is emphasized by taped lines on the floor.) Behind Man 2 and Girl are projection screens; behind Man 1, the wall of television sets. Each continues his activity: Man 1's unwrapped hand begins to pulse, twitch, and finally, to scuttle away as if it had a life of its own, and he strikes it with the other hand. (This "all three" shot to be from directly above.)

A film, projected in very slow motion, replaces the live images: A large number of people (at a theatre, sporting event, etc.) applauding. The chosen excerpt should have a certain build, development, and ending. During the remainder of the Happening, sequential segments of it are inserted—always, as this initial one, quite brief and in slow motion—until the shot is complete.

GIRL: Switches on tape recorder. A male voice is heard lecturing on the anatomy of the hand, and the girl mimes the words as if she were speaking them. Rear projection on the screen behind her presents words and diagrams as they are written in chalk (although no hand is visible) on a blackboard. When the speech ends, the Girl switches off the recorder.

MAN 2: On the screen behind Man 2's table an excerpt from *The Beast With Five Fingers* is projected showing an amputated hand crawling along the floor. Perhaps Man 2 can be seen at the projector.

Applause film continued. Slow motion.

GIRL: During this section (until the next film segment), Girl may be making noises by moving her hands, fingernails, etc. in various ways close to and on the microphone. If so, her picture is occasionally split-imaged in one corner.

MAN 1: Using scissors held in right hand, cuts rubber or plastic glove off of (what appears to be) left hand raised to shoulder height (actually plaster hand with false "sleeve" matching suit material). When glove falls away, hand is seen to be black. Camera pulls back slightly to show false sleeve.

MAN 2: Cuts glove off of "left hand." The hand is broken plaster, and as each piece comes free it rises out of the top of the frame. (Man 2 is actually hanging upside down, and the camera image is inverted.)

MAN 1: Holds plaster hand, fingers toward the table, and pours clear water into it.

Removes small plug from one finger, and dark liquid pours out, staining white tablecloth.

MAN 2: Holds plaster hand upright. Removes plug from finger, and dark water pours out of the top of screen. (Man 2 is still upside down.)

MAN 1: Closeup of Man 1's hand on table. Blasts of "snow" hit it; it twitches, camera pulls back to show Man 1 spraying his own hand with Christmas snow from a pressurized can. The hand is covered.

MAN 2: Seated with plaster hands apparently rising on thin supports behind him. (Actually Man 2 is still inverted, and the hands are hanging.) His own hands, held in a semi-clasped position in front of his chest, jerk and twitch spasmodically. At each movement, one of the background hands (its cord cut) rises out of the top of the frame. The camera pulls back and corrects the image, showing Man 2 inverted and the strings being cut.

Applause film continued. Slow motion.

GIRL: Stands with hand out to side, fingers spread. Its shadow falls on screen. Camera pulls back to show Man 1 at overhead projector, He draws her hand so that drawing is projected on hand. (Perhaps split screen here: Closeups of drawing and of Girl's hand with drawing on it.) When drawing is finished, she removes her hand, and the image is projected onto the screen, replacing shadow.

MAN 2: Seated at table, a piece of paper under what appears to be his empty left sleeve, he draws a hand where the "missing" one should be. Perhaps he pulls the paper along and draws several.

GIRL: Closeup of her face with hands, palm out, against cheeks. Films are projected on one hand, then on the other: Cars, planes, trains, etc. on the right; charts, maps, etc. on the left. Occasionally she turns a hand in as if to look at the images. The camera pulls back, showing Man 1 and Man 2 operating 8 mm. projectors.

Applause film continued. Slow motion.

MAN 1, MAN 2, GIRL: Nails finger of rubber-glovelike hand to table, stretches rubber, nails again, etc.

Man 2 plays hand-shaped rattle and Girl plays hand flute (one tube of a guitar pitch pipe inserted into the tip of each finger of a hollow plaster hand) during this image. Their pictures are split-screened.

Applause film continued. Slow motion.

GIRL: Hands cut from paper and hanging from threads are blown against her by a strong fan. When they hit, they stick.

MAN 2: Liquid apparently pours from his left hand into a goblet on the table. (A hidden tube runs down his sleeve.) When glass is full, he drinks.

GIRL: Cuts the threads of clinging hands with scissors. Fan still on.

MAN 1: Holds white (apparently plaster) hand. Bites it, cuts it into sections, and eats some. (It is chocolate.)

GIRL: Pulls paper hands off one at a time. They rise out of the top of the frame. (She is hanging upside down and the camera image is inverted.) The fan is still blowing.

Applause film continued. Slow motion.

MAN 1: Pours boiling water over semitransparent hand. It dissolves. (It is cast in gelatin.)

MAN 2: Holds hand mounted upright on small box. Smoke rises from the fingertips.

GIRL: Places left hand in a large dish and pours a viscous white liquid over it until it is covered. Holds up hand, letting liquid drip off. Repeats procedure with other hand while all three performers appear in split-screen.

Applause film continues, slow motion. It concludes.

MAN 1, MAN 2, GIRL: Each, in sequence, lights plaster hand. Camera pulls back to show all three hands burning. (Similar to opening establishing shot. From above. Lights should be dimmed.)

MAN 1: Seated at table, looking at hand. He stands, raises hand and slams it down, shattering it. (It is made of plaster.)

MAN 2: Film projected on Man 2's screen (no performer can be seen): Scattered pieces of plaster move together to form a hand.

MAN 1, MAN 2, GIRL: All three performers, their backs to camera, stand watching television wall. When broken hand reassembles on "ten second delay" screens, the image freezes. The same thing happens when "twenty second delay" screens reach that point: All screens show the same image. Performers turn to camera, smile, and bow.

END

Although I was concentrating primarily on my sculpture, I did other Happenings during 1964 and 1965. They were more or less similar to *Hand Happening*, systematically developing specific images or concepts through a variety of technical means. All of these pieces made use of what I have called "non-matrixed" performing: As in the *Hand Happening*, the performers were merely themselves doing certain actions and no imaginary characters or places were created. In defining Happenings, I had considered this one of the most important and characteristic elements. Then in 1966, I did a performance that made extensive use of acting. It was called *Room 706;* the following description appeared in *The Drama Review.*

Room 706

The title *Room 706* refers to the large lecture hall on the seventh floor of Saint Francis College, Brooklyn, New York, in which the piece was presented. Although the following description is intended partly as a guide for anyone wishing to re-create the work, the title and almost everything else in such a re-creation—the dialogue, the structure, possibly even the physical setup—would change. As was indicated when such a re-creation was presented in Argentina, based only on a vocal description, the "integrity" of the piece lies not in the particular words and images used in the original performance, but in the concept and the manner in which the material is generated.

The first step in presenting *Room 706* was to make a short black-and-white lip-sync film, using a single-system Auricon, of an impromptu discussion of plans for the performance by its three prime movers. The conversation was also tape-recorded and then transcribed to make up the basic script used in the performance.

Room 706 was presented twice, on March 4th and 5th, 1966. The playing space was the shape of an equilateral triangle in the middle of the large rectangular room. The audience was seated in rows of folding chairs along the three sides. At each vertex of the triangle (A, B, C) was a table (with tape recorder) and two chairs. Directly behind each table was a portable motion picture screen. Three similar tables were arranged to form another triangle at the center of the playing area, and on them were placed two motion picture projectors, two slide projectors, an opaque projector, and an overhead projector. Colored spotlights—each vertex table had its own color—projected from boom-standards behind each audience section. The spotlights were controlled from a portable switchboard placed on the stage at one end of the room. The board and its operator were visible throughout the performance, as was all other technical activity: there was no "offstage."

The performance was divided into twenty-two discrete parts, as indicated by numbers below, clearly punctuated by blackouts.

1. The house lights were turned off, and performance spotlights flashed on and off three times, remaining on the last time. At this cue, a man standing at each of the three vertex tables started a tape recorder. The machines "spoke to each other": each machine broadcast the voice of one man—actually, as the audience would later confirm, that of the man who now stood silently at each table—and the three recorded voices "played" the basic scene.

KIRBY: OK, let's get the time in, first of all. Check the time.

FERLAZZO: Oh, it's-a-a—Exactly? 10, 11, 12, 13. . . .

KIRBY: Well, I've got it up there, 1:15 OK. So we'll run for three minutes.

FERLAZZO: All right.

KIRBY: OK. Now the first thing we've got to do is—how about the lights? Technical thing . . .

FERLAZZO: Is that thing running now?

KIRBY: Yeah, it's running.

FERLAZZO: Why don't we . . . All right, all right, you can judge from that three minutes. All right.

KIRBY: Now we've got to get lights for this thing.

FERLAZZO: Yeah, now . . . How about the spots downstairs, Brother? Are they good? Did that man ever return them?

BROTHER ANTHELM: Oh, they're all back. Some of them have to be rewired now. We've only got three that are in any working condition at all.

FERLAZZO: Uhuh. Three?

BRO. ANTHELM: Now if you want to use the ones . . . the ones I call the Klieg lights. . . .

FERLAZZO: Yeah.

BRO. ANTHELM: There's only three of them working, but how about the ones we used for our own production?

FERLAZZO: Yeah, but we'd have to bring up all the stands then and all that, huh?

BRO. ANTHELM: All right, the others are easier to handle, but they do not have any controls. They're not on . . . rheostats.

FERLAZZO: Yeah, that's right. Yeah. Uhuh. Well—a—who—who's that guy, the janitor?

BRO. ANTHELM: Fred Wilkin.

FERLAZZO: Wilkin. Yeah. I spoke to him, and he has—a—the things that we did for—for—Kirby's last—last thing in the lounge, *Man Seasons?*

KIRBY: I'd rather get those spots if we can get them. Can we get them?

FERLAZZO: Spots?

BRO. ANTHELM: Yeah, they're available. They're there.

KIRBY: Just rig them on poles, the way they were for the productions, with a switchboard or something.

FERLAZZO: Yeah.

KIRBY: Because I'd like to do some complicated lighting, if we can work it out.

BRO. ANTHELM: Well, they're just sitting there. You might as well use them. We're not going into production . . .

KIRBY: OK. It could be, but Paul said that perhaps it would be difficult to get them out . . . because you see what I want to do is to . . . This is Room 706, right?

FERLAZZO: Yeah.

KIRBY: With entrance here and the doorway here . . . would be to seat . . . We have screens at either end—we'll buy white paper for it . . .

FERLAZZO: Yeah.

KIRBY: And then seat the audience . . .

FERLAZZO: Uhuh. I see. Yeah.

KIRBY: So then we'll need to light the areas . . . maybe five areas.

FERLAZZO: Yeah, but have we got four poles?

BRO. ANTHELM: We've got four poles. That could be your four sections. We could run the wires over to here—the only thing is stepping on them coming in and out, but . . .

FERLAZZO: Well, that's . . . that's all right. We've done that before. Yeah.

BRO. ANTHELM: It's never been a tremendous problem. Put your—a—dimmer over here, with someone to operate it, and that's it.

KIRBY: Now, now, how about the acting? You're, you're all set to appear in the performance? Right? Live?

BRO. ANTHELM: All right.

FERLAZZO: Yeah. Yeah. (*Laughs.*)

KIRBY: You all agree to that? OK. We'll be doing the same thing that we're doing right now.

2. The basic sound film was projected on the screen at Vertex A. In the film, Brother Anthelm Drowne sat behind a large desk in the office of the Saint Francis College library, and Paul Ferlazzo sat in a chair in front of the desk; Michael Kirby, although heard, was unseen at first, moving to the desk part way through the film to make a sketch of the proposed setup and then disappearing again behind the camera. The dialogue, of course, was exactly the same as that heard from the three tape recorders in Part 1, but now the audience could see the speakers.

3. High up on the stage near the switchboard, the head and shoulders of a man in a black tuxedo were illuminated by flashlight as he stood on a ladder. Reading from a card, he said (for example):

The time is now 3:45 P.M., Friday, March 4th, 1966. This is the third part of the performance. There will be twenty-two parts in all. The performance will last about fifty minutes.

4. On the screen at Vertex B a list of names was flashed with the opaque projector:

ROOM 706 by Michael Kirby
performed by:
Bro. Anthelm Drowne, O.S.F.
Nicholas Caccavo
Joseph Campanaro
Thomas Crotty

Thomas Downes
Paul Ferlazzo
Lawrence Hayes
John Heslin
Henry Kelly
Michael Kirby
Thomas Laquercia
Edwin MacDonald
Clifford Mylett

As soon as the projector went on, the performers began to move into and across the performance space. Those who had not been involved previously had been sitting in the audience or standing behind the spectators. The man in the tuxedo read the title, and each performer in turn stopped and read his name.

5.   On the screen at Vertex C a black-and-white film was projected. It showed the exterior of the building in which the performance was taking place: just as the spectators had probably done, the camera walked toward the pillared entrance, glanced at the bronze sign reading "Saint Francis College," and passed into the lobby as the door swung open. The camera moved toward the elevators, a hand pushed the "up" button, the doors slid open, and the camera entered the car. Indicator lights in the elevator were shown flashing in sequence until the seventh floor, where the doors slid open, and the camera walked to the room where the performance was held. At the same time, on the screen at Vertex B, the opaque projector threw the enlargement of an instructional folder: "How to reach Saint Francis College." A small moving arrow pointed out the college on a map of Brooklyn.

   On the screen at Vertex A, a man at the overhead projector was drawing a plan of the room.

6.   At Vertex A, the three men who had turned on the tape recorders and had appeared in the basic film acted the basic

scene. The table, of course, represented the office desk, and the men were dressed just as they had been when the film was made. While they acted the original film was shown without sound on the screen behind their table.

7. At Vertex B, the man in the tuxedo read:

It should be noted that the terms "scene," or even "hermetic scene," and "compartment" are not the same. "Scene" has primary reference to people and to place. A scene is "played" between actors and by an actor. A "French scene" begins and ends with the entrance or exit of a major character. But many units in Happenings contain only sounds or physical elements, and not performers. Frequently, although performers are in physical proximity, there is no interplay between them, and an imaginary place is seldom established. [Michael Kirby, *Happenings*, E. P. Dutton & Co., p. 14.]

This is Part 7. There will be fifteen more parts.

8. Drawing on the overhead projector, a man outlined one of the many bas-relief pillars that decorated the walls. The enlarged marks of his pencil were thrown directly onto the pillar, and when the outline was complete, he slowly shifted the machine so that the image separated entirely from its "original" and could be compared. At the same time, two men with slide projectors were throwing negative photographs of various portions of the room onto the walls and ceiling. Holding the projectors in their hands, they slowly moved the pictures until they reached that part of the room shown in the slide. Then they switched off the light, put a new slide in place, and repeated the procedure.

9. The machine which had been projecting the basic film faced toward Vertex A, but now the beam was reflected in a mirror so that the picture (reversed image) fell on the screen at Vertex B. While the basic film played without sound above them, three men who had not previously taken part in the performance (except for reading their names from the "program") acted out the scene. Their positions and blocking were

also reversed: when the man playing "Kirby" made the diagram, he drew with his left hand.

10.   Standing on a chair in the central projection complex, the man in the tuxedo, lit only by a light from below, again read from a card:

The length of this room, Room 706, is forty-seven feet, and its width is thirty-five feet.

This is Part number 10 of the performance. Twelve more parts will follow.

11.   A black-and-white film taken at rehearsal of the piece was projected on the screen at Vertex C. Although the rehearsal had taken place in the same room, all of the performers were not wearing the same clothing as they did in the actual presentation, and, of course, there was no audience. The film, taken chronologically and composed of many brief shots edited in the camera by Richard Benter, showed elements of the performance that the spectators had already seen and then images yet to come. It included closeups of performers, of physical details of the room such as the clock and the crucifix, of the projection and sound equipment in operation, and a self-portrait of the cameraman.

At the same time, the opaque projector threw the image of the typewritten script for the basic scene onto the screen at Vertex B.

On the screen at Vertex A, the audience could watch a diagram of the actors' positions and movements being drawn on the overhead projector.

12.   Four men, who had not been involved in the performance since the introductory "program," began to act at Vertex C. Although similar to the basic scene at first, this was a new scene. The script was taken from a tape recording of a rehearsal of the actors who had performed the "mirror image" of the basic scene at Vertex B in Part 9. That is, three of the

new men were playing actors during a rehearsal, and one was playing the director: the material being rehearsed was the basic scene.

LAQUERCIA: "OK, let's get the time in, first of all. Check the time."

CAMPANARO: "Oh, it's exactly—a—10, 11, 12, 13 . . ."

LAQUERCIA: "Well, I've got it up there. 1:15, OK. So we'll run for three minutes."

CAMPANARO: "All right."

LAQUERCIA: "OK . . ."

KIRBY: What, what do you mean by that: "We'll run for three minutes"?

LAQUERCIA: Well, the . . . the . . . Yer gonna hafta have— the camera's going to—a—operate for three minutes. You're gonna stop the thing.

KIRBY: Right. It's about a hundred feet of film, and that was what we were going on the basis of—a hundred feet of film. You're leaving out the "—a—a—."

LAQUERCIA: And you're not making a question of "Exactly."

KIRBY: Joe? It's "—a—a—." He's looking at the watch here.

CAMPANARO: Alrighty. Right.

KIRBY: And then, after you've looked at the watch, you say, "Exactly? You want it in seconds?"

CAMPANARO: OK. Right.

LAQUERCIA: "OK, let's get the time in, first of all. Check the time."

CAMPANARO: "Oh, it's—a—a—Exactly? 10, 11, 12, 13 . . ."

KIRBY (*simultaneously*): That's it!

LAQUERCIA: "Well, I've got it up there. 1:15. OK. So we'll run for three minutes."

CAMPANARO: "All right."

LAQUERCIA: "OK. Now the first thing we've got to do is—how about the lights? Technical things . . ."

CAMPANARO: "Is that thing running *now?*"

KIRBY: What are you talking about?

CAMPANARO: The camera.

KIRBY: Yes. He didn't know it was on. OK. Don't rush, Tom.

LAQUERCIA: Oh, OK.—a—shall we—again from the top?

KIRBY: No no. Go ahead.

LAQUERCIA: Well, we . . .

KIRBY: He says, "Is that thing running now?"

LAQUERCIA: "Yeah, it's running."

CAMPANARO: "Why don't we . . . All right, all right, you can judge from that three minutes. All right."

LAQUERCIA: "Now we've got to get the lights for this thing."

CAMPANARO: "Yeah, now how about that . . ."

KIRBY: Now, you say . . . you say this to Paul. You're telling him—we've discussed this beforehand about needing the lights, and he's told me that it may be a difficult thing to get them out of the basement. Now you're telling him to ask Brother about the lights. It's in the way you say the line. You say, "Let's get down to business. Ask Brother about the lights . . . because he hasn't been in the conversation yet." And he picks you up on that. He gets the message.

LAQUERCIA: "Now we get the . . . Now we've got to get the lights for this thing."

CAMPANARO: "Yeah now, how about the spots downstairs, Brother? Are they good? Did that man ever return them?"

DiCLEMENTI: "Oh, they're all back. Some of them have to be rewired now. We've got only three that are in any working condition at all."

CAMPANARO: "Uhuh."

KIRBY: Now "that man . . . that man," I think, was the . . . pastor down on the corner.

LAQUERCIA: Glenesk.

KIRBY: I think so. I think that's what Paul said. And that he borrowed the lights. I think. And Paul thought that he still had them.

LAQUERCIA: Pardon me, can I ask you one thing right now? Where did you ever get this dialogue? Did you just sit down and turn on the tape recorder and then copy it from the tape recorder?

KIRBY: We shot it. It's a virtual thing. I . . . it's on the tape, and we also recorded it. So this is exactly what we say in the movie . . .

LAQUERCIA: Oh, I see.

KIRBY: . . . which is now being processed.

13. At Vertex A, the man in the tuxedo again read from a card (the numbers have been invented, but the audience did not exceed 150 at either performance):

The attendance this evening is 108.
This total is made up of eighty-three men, twenty-four women, and one child.

This is Part 13 of twenty-two parts.

14. A motion-picture closeup of Kirby's face looking straight at the camera and saying the first line of the basic scene ap-

peared on the screen at Vertex A. During the moment of darkness after the image clicked off, the beam of the projector was reflected with a mirror onto the screen at Vertex B, and Ferlazzo's face clicked on there, speaking the second line. (Light on the optical soundtrack at the beginning and end of each "take" with an Auricon camera causes a click. In this case the noises were not edited out and added a kind of harsh rhythm to the section.) When it was Brother Anthelm's turn to speak, the image of his face was reflected onto the screen at Vertex C. About half of the dialogue of the basic scene was presented in this manner, each of the three actors always speaking in closeups from his "own" screen.

15.   The "rehearsal" scene was again acted by the four performers at Vertex C. When they were a short way into the scene, they were stopped by a man (Kirby) from the basic acting group and given directions about movement and interpretation. The four resumed acting at a designated point in the dialogue, and, after a moment or so, the area lights went out, ending the section.

16.   At Vertex B the man in the tuxedo read:

This does not mean that there is always a clear line between matrixed and non-matrixed performing. The terms refer to polar conceptions which are quite obvious in their pure forms, but a continuum exists between them, and it is possible that this or that performance might be difficult to categorize. In other words, the strength of character-place matrices may be described as "strong" or "weak" and the exact point at which a weak matrix becomes non-matrix is not easy to perceive. But even in the extreme case in which both the work of the performer and the information provided by his context are so vague and nonspecific that we could not explain "who" he was or "where" he was supposed to be, we often feel that he is someone other than himself or in some place other than the actual place of performance. We know when we are suspending disbelief or being asked to suspend it. [Michael Kirby, *Tulane Drama Review*, Winter, 1965, p. 27.]

There are six more parts to the performance.

17.   Once again, the rehearsal scene began at Vertex C. When the actors reached the point where they had been stopped previously, one of them reached over and switched on the tape recorder on the table. The four listened again to the director's voice and to their own responses and questions. (When he began the live rehearsal in Part 15, the director had put the machine on "record" and then, when he was finished, had rewound the tape so it would be ready to be played in this part.) The live acting, responding to the instructions which had come from the recorder, resumed again briefly before the section ended.

18.   The basic scene was "played" by motion-picture close-ups of two of the actors, Brother Anthelm and Kirby, and one live actor, Paul Ferlazzo. The film images moved slowly over the walls and ceiling, appearing in unexpected places and disappearing, clicking on and off, and Ferlazzo walked around the triangular playing area speaking to them. About half the basic scene was presented in this way with the film actors talking "with" the live one.

19.   The lights for all three acting areas were turned on. Performers remained in their own areas, but each now played the basic scene with one man from each of the other two areas. (The "director" at Vertex C did not participate.) All three versions of the scene played at the same time: before responding to his cue each actor waited while two other lines —one from each of the other two scenes—were spoken. Each scene began at a different point in the dialogue. The following is an *example* of the effect (letters indicate playing area vertex and names indicate character, not actor):

A—KIRBY: OK, let's get the time in first of all. Check the time.

   B—BRO. ANTHELM: There's only three of them working, but how about the ones we used for our own production?

C—FERLAZZO: Wilkin. Yeah. I spoke to him, and he has—a—the things that we did for—for—Kirby's last—last thing in the lounge, *Man Seasons?*

B—FERLAZZO: Oh, it's—a—a—Exactly? 10, 11, 12, 13. . . .

A—FERLAZZO: Yeah, but we'd have to bring up all the stands then and all that, huh?

B—KIRBY: I'd rather use the spots if we can get them. Can we get them?

20. During this part each performer fuctioned independently: he had been instructed to take two or three steps in any direction, say any line or fragment of a line from the piece, remain motionless for a few seconds, and then repeat the procedure, moving in a different direction. The men could move anywhere within the performance area. At first the lines were merely mimed so that the image was silent: after a while they were spoken out loud, and the voices "built" and sometimes overlapped. One at a time the actors moved out of the playing area, until only the man in the tuxedo was left.

21. Using the opaque projector, the man in the tuxedo threw enlargements of three polaroid photographs he had taken and developed during Part 19 onto the screen at Vertex B. They were pictures of the spectators: one photograph of each audience group.

22. Turning off the opaque projector—there was no blackout between the last two parts—the man in the tuxedo switched on a tape recorder and walked out of the playing area. On the tape, the volume turned up, was the sound of enthusiastic applause.

In *Room 706* I was attempting, for one thing, to use acting not for the meaning it could convey, but for its pure experiential qualities—in the same way, so to speak, that paint has been used for *its* qualities of hue, texture, and so forth without the necessity of representing anything. In order to do this I tried to make the basic scene as close to real life as I could. The dialogue was not composed but was "found" in a situation that approximated an everyday one. The actors were playing themselves and not characters whose inner natures they would have to imagine or invent. In other versions of the scene, however, additional levels of unreality were added so that the quality of acting, in *itself*, might become clear.

(Of course, another aspect of *Room 706* was its explicit relationship to the particular space where it was performed. In this sense, it was quite similar to my "embedded" sculpture, and many of the same comments apply to both. The sculpture is discussed in the next chapter.)

Since 1966, all of my performances have made extensive use of acting. If I have to use a generic term more specific than "performance," I refer to them as "alogical plays" rather than "Happenings." The structure is similar to that of a Happening and is obviously derived from it, but the acting makes the result significantly different.

In May, 1966, I did a performance called *The Chekov Machine* at the New York State University College at Oneonta. It made use of, among other things, three short scenes from three different plays by Anton Chekov. All of the verbal material, therefore, had a consistent texture or quality, but the scenes, which were treated somewhat similarly to the acted scenes in *Room 706,* did not explain each other or develop an information structure.

A 1967 performance at the Fashion Institute of Technology combined a scene that was "found" in life by means of a concealed tape recorder and a modified scene from *Hamlet* ("Will you play upon this pipe?" and "Do you see yonder cloud that's almost in the shape of a camel?"). In a performance presented at Bennington College (April 23, 1967) and at the Youth Pavilion, Expo 67, a single scene from *The White Devil* by John Webster was used. Since I was staging the work myself, scattered notes and script fragments were sufficient, and the following script description is "after the fact." The piece was conceived for my brother E. T. (Ted) Kirby and me: We are identical twins. The production was revised slightly after the Bennington performance (called *Bennington Alogical*), and the order of images given here is that used at the Youth Pavilion. The actresses who performed at both Bennington and Expo were Anna Cronin, Linda Feldman, and Elizabeth Johnson; John Secor was technical director.

Expo Alogical

Because of the manner in which projections are used, the performance is presented in a proscenium or modified proscenium arrangement in which the spectators all view it from more or less the same angle. A motion-picture screen forms a backdrop to the shallow playing area. Tape recorders are placed at Left, Right, and Center Stage, near the edge of the apron.

The twins, when they appear, are not dressed exactly alike: One wears a black suit and turtleneck jersey, the other a less formal black jacket, trousers, and turtleneck. Each of the girls wears a distinctive monochrome dress or coat that helps to identify her in the color slide and film sequences.

The performance is divided into nine sequential images or compartments, each represented by a number in the following description, that are separated by blackouts.

1.   All five actors wear latex life masks of the twin(s). When the lights come on, an actress wearing a life mask is at each of the three tape recorders. They push the "play" buttons simultaneously, and the machines "talk to each other." The only sounds on the tapes are the voices of the performers speaking lines from the basic scene of the play (an excerpt from *The White Devil* by John Webster, the complete dialogue of which is given in section 4). The progression in the sound sequences is toward decreasing comprehensibility.

For the performances I staged, I used only the questions and their answers, if any, from the basic scene. In the opening tape sequence, the center machine spoke Flamineo's questions and answers, the left machine spoke Vittoria's, and the right machine spoke Zanche's. There were twenty separate questions and answers. As can be seen from the following example, the scene itself could not be understood from this limited material.

Left recorder	*Center recorder*	*Right recorder*
"What do you want? What would you have me do?"		
	"I made a vow to my deceased lord . . ."	
"Did he enjoin it?"		
	"He did." ". . . what hope, then, for us?"	
"Do you mean to die indeed?"		
	"With as much pleasure as e'er my father gat me."	
"Are you grown atheist?		
		"Do you think that I'll outlive you?"

In the second sequence on the tapes, a voice from one machine asked a question, and a voice from another echoed it, comparing the voice qualities and line readings of the performers. For example:

Left recorder	Center recorder	Right recorder
	(left twin) ". . . what hope, then, for us?"	
		(right twin) ". . . what hope, then, for us?"
	(left twin) ". . . what hope, then, for us?"	
(right twin) ". . . what hope, then, for us?"		
(right twin) ". . . what hope, then, for us?"	(left twin) ". . . what hope, then, for us?"	(right twin) ". . . what hope, then, for us?"
(left twin) "Are you ready?"	(right twin) "Are you ready?"	(left twin) "Are you ready?"
(left twin) "Are you ready?"		
	(right twin) "Are you ready?"	
		(left twin) "Are you ready?"
	(right twin) "Are you ready?"	

In the final tape sequence, the beginnings and ends of the question-and-answer phrases were eliminated by rerecording and editing, so that they lost intelligibility. They were blended into each other. The same fragment was repeated several or many times. At times all three machines spoke, while at other times only one or two could be heard. The treatment was "musical."

While the tape recorders play, the twins, also wearing life

masks, are illuminated center stage. Facing each other, they perform a double-mirror "dance" or "theatre game."

First one is the "mirror" and copies the other's movements and positions, and then the other twin becomes the "mirror." (With enough practice it is possible to reach the point where both are "mirrors" and neither feels he is originating the movement.) The movement is slow, simple, non-indicative, and "ritualized." There may be sections of stasis.

2. In preparing this section, slides and motion pictures are made of each actor performing selected simple movements taken from or based on the movements occurring in the basic scene. Three movements for the men and three for the women are sufficient.

The film is projected onto the center of the screen with a series of slides projected at each side: When all three projectors are on, there are three evenly spaced illuminated rectangles. The figures that appear in the projected pictures are exactly life size. The pictures appear and disappear simultaneously, remaining on for seven seconds and off, leaving the stage in darkness, for four seconds; slightly longer periods of darkness indicate the division of the whole sequence into smaller structural units. At times both the slide projectors and the motion-picture projector merely throw white light onto the screen, revealing a live actor who has stepped into position during the preceding moment of darkness and who performs one of the same actions that appear in the photographs. In this way, comparisons are presented between, for example, the live actor performing a movement, the same movement as it appears in film, and a stage in that movement "frozen" in a slide.

In *Expo Alogical* the sequence was divided into five subsections: Each actress had her own part, the twins were seen in the same part, and all the actors appeared live in the final part. The men's movements were: raising a pistol, aiming toward the audience, and, in the last two parts, firing (shoots); falling as if shot (falls). The women's movements were shooting, gesturing toward heaven with both hands and looking up, and kneeling. The fourth section is given below as an example:

SLIDE PROJECTOR	FILM PROJECTOR	SLIDE PROJECTOR
falls	falls	falls
falls	falls	falls
(*twin appears live in remaining units*)		(*twin appears live in remaining units*)
falls	falls	falls
shoots	falls	shoots
	(*film in remaining units is negative*)	
shoots	falls	shoots
shoots	falls	shoots
falls	falls	falls

3. The basic scene is filmed with one twin playing the first part (until Zanche's first line) with one of the actresses and the other twin completing the scene (after Zanche's "entrance") with the other two actresses. The film is then cut into equal segments of about thirty-seconds duration, and it is spliced together in a new order: Segments involving one twin are alternated with segments involving the other twin, and the overall continuity of each twin's part is altered.

In performance the first segment of film is shown at center. There is no sound. When the segment ends, the projector is shut off, and what the audience has just seen on film is acted by the same performers at one side of the stage using the dialogue. Then the next segment, which involves the other twin, is shown, and the actors at the other side of the stage perform it. In this way, alternating silent film and live performances at both sides of the stage, the whole scene is presented in a radically revised order.

4. For the first time, the basic scene from *The White Devil*—the source of the performance material in the preceding (and succeeding) sections—is presented more or less completely and in its proper chronology. But rather than being acted by a man and two women, it is played by the twins and a life-sized dummy built to resemble the twins. Wearing a life mask or head of the twins' features, the dummy is supported by one or two of the girls and "acts" in synchronization with a tape recording of one of the twins' voices speaking Flamineo's lines. Rather than impersonating women, the twins speak slightly altered lines: The gender is changed in the "'I made a vow to my deceased lord" passages, "Gentle madam" becomes "Kind sir," and so forth. The basic scene, without these slight alterations but modified as it was used in *Expo Alogical,* is as follows:

FROM *The White Devil* ACT V SC. VI

FLAM.—Flamineo; VIT. C.—Vittoria Corombona; ZAN.—Zanche

FLAM.: Look, these are better far at a dead lift than all your jewel-house.

VIT. C.: And yet, methinks, these stones have no air luster, they are ill set.

FLAM.: I'll turn the right side towards you: you shall see how they will sparkle.

VIT. C.: Turn this horror from me! What do you want? What would you have me do?

FLAM.: I made a vow to my deceased lord, neither yourself nor I should outlive him the numbering of four hours.

VIT. C.: Did he enjoin it?

FLAM.: He did; and 'twas a deadly jealousy, lest any should enjoy thee after him, that urged him vow me to it. For my death, I did propose it voluntarily, knowing, if he could not be safe in his own court, being a great Duke, what hope, then, for us?

VIT. C.: This is your melancholy and despair.

FLAM.: My life hath done service to other men; my death shall serve mine own turn. Make you ready.

VIT. C.: Do you mean to die indeed?

FLAM.: With as much plesure as e'er my father gat me.

VIT. C.: Are you grown atheist? Will you turn your body, which is the goodly palace of the soul, to the soul's slaughter-house? I prithee, yet remember, millions are now in their graves, which at last day like mandrakes shall rise shriek-ing.

ZAN.: Gentle madam, seem to consent, only persuade him teach the way to death; let him die first.

VIT. C.: 'Tis good. I apprehend it.
O, but frailty! Yet I am now resolved; farewell, affliction! Behold, Brachiano, I that while you lived did make a flaming altar of my heart to sacrifice unto you, now am ready to sacrifice heart and all. Farewell, Zanche!

ZAN.: How, madam! Do you think that I'll outlive you; espe-cially when my best self, Flamineo, goes the same voyage?

FLAM.: O, most lovéd Moor!

ZAN.: Only by all my love let me entreat you,—since it is most necessary one of us do violence to ourselves, let you or I be her sad taster, teach her how to die.

FLAM.: Thou dost instruct me nobly: take these pistols, because my hand is stained with blood already: one of these you shall level at my breast, the other 'gainst your own, and so we'll die most equally contented: but first swear not to outlive me.

VIT. & ZAN.: Most religiously.

FLAM.: Then here's an end of me; farewell, daylight! These are two cupping-glasses that shall draw all my infected blood out. Are you ready?

VIT. & ZAN.: Ready.

FLAM.: Whither shall I go now? Whether I resolve to fire, earth, water, air, or all the elements by scruples, I know not, nor greatly care. Shoot, shoot: of all deaths the violent death is best, for from ourselves it steals ourselves so fast, the pain, once apprehended is quite past.

(They shoot; he falls; and they run to him, and tread upon him.)

VIT. C.: What, are you dropt?

FLAM.: I am mixed with earth already: as you are noble, perform your vows, and bravely follow me.

VIT. C.: Whither? To hell?

ZAN.: To most assured damnation?

VIT. C.: O thou most curséd devil!

ZAN.: Thou art caught in thine own engine. I tread the fire out that would have been my ruin.

FLAM.: Will you be perjured?

VIT. C.: Think whither thou art going.

ZAN.: And remember what villainies thou hast acted.

VIT. C.: This thy death shall make me like a blazing ominous star: look up and tremble.

FLAM.: O, the way's dark and horrible. I cannot see: Shall I have no company?

VIT. C.: O, yes, thy sins do run before thee to fetch fire from hell, to light thee thither.

FLAM.: There's a plumber laying pipes in my guts, it scalds—
Wilt thou outlive me?

ZAN.: Yes, and drive a stake through thy body; for we'll give
it out that thou didst this violence upon thyself.

FLAM.: O cunning devils! Now I have tried your love . . . I
am not wounded. (*rises*.) The pistols held no bullets: 'twas
a plot to prove your kindness to me; and I live to punish
your ingratitude.

5. (*During this section positive and/or negative projected
slide images of the basic scene slowly move horizontally across
the screen and proscenium walls from both directions.*)
At one side of the stage one twin and one of the actresses
play the first part of the basic scene; at the other side of the
stage the other twin and the other two actresses play the remainder of the scene. Although the two groups act simultaneously, the lines do not overlap or conflict: Before "picking up"
the cue for a line of dialogue, each actor waits until he has
heard a line spoken by a performer in the other group. An attempt is made to "hold the pauses" through concentration and
movement, so that the impression of alternation is minimized
and the quality of simultaneity is maximized. When a group
finishes its portion of the script, it begins again until a pre-
determined signal ends the section.

A brief example of the use of dialogue in this section follows:

Left group *Right group*

(FLAMINEO)
Look, these are better far
at a dead lift than all
your jewel-house.

(ZANCHE)
Gentle madam, seem to
consent, only persuade
him teach the way to death,
let him die first.

Left group	Right group
(VIT. C.) And yet, methinks, these stones have no air luster, they are ill set.	
	(VIT. C.) 'Tis good. I apprehend it. O, but frailty! Yet I am now resolved; farewell affliction! Behold, Brachiano, I that while you lived did make a flaming altar of my heart to sacrifice unto you, now am ready to sacrifice heart and all. Farewell, Zanche!
(FLAM.) I'll turn the right side towards you: you shall see how they will sparkle.	
	(ZAN.) How, madam! Do you think that I'll outlive you; especially when my best self, Flamineo, goes the same voyage?
(VIT. C.) Turn this horror from me! What do you want? What would you have me do?	
	(FLAM.) O, most lovèd Moor!

6.   One of the twins talks directly to the audience, telling them the source of the basic scene, the date of its writing, how it relates to the play as a whole, and any other facts that he thinks are interesting or appropriate about *The White Devil*, John Webster, or Elizabethan playwriting in general.

Then he begins to direct the other twin and one of the actresses in a rehearsal of the scene. The acting is intermittent as
the "director" stops the scene to talk about the characters and
situation, offer suggestions on line interpretation and movement, and answer questions.

The rehearsal is recorded on tape by the other two actresses
who independently, but more or less alternately, record a portion of what is being said, rewind the tape, and play it back.
Thus one machine records not only the extemporaneous rehearsal but the sounds of the voices broadcast by the other
machine. The density and volume of these overlapping voices
is increased until the end of the section.

7. The three actresses stand facing the audience. The film
image of the face of one of the twins appears at some point in
the theatre, speaking Flamineo's opening line. The face disappears while the first actress answers it with Vittoria Corombona's line. It appears again at another spot giving Flamineo's
second line. The second actress responds to what it says. Part
or all of the scene is played in this fashion, with the three actresses taking turns at speaking the female lines to the film
image that moves across the walls and ceiling, appears at unexpected spots, and so forth.

8. A tape recording of the basic scene is played on the machine
at the center of the apron. It either repeats several times or, if
a shorter image is desired, begins in the middle of the scene and
plays through to the middle again. All five performers simultaneously act the scene in synchronization with the taped voices.
They may either pantomime silently, letting the tape speak
"for" them, or they may use any degree or type of vocal volume
and expressiveness, varying or switching styles of delivery in
the middle of passages, if they desire. The actors should listen
to the overall sound as if it were a musical composition and
work spontaneously with the given material as jazz musicians
might do. The twins perform Flamineo at opposite sides of the
stage, and the actresses, who know the roles of both Vittoria

Corombona and Zanche, play whichever part they wish with whichever twin they choose, switching from one role to the other and from one playing area to the other at will. Thus all three actresses might, at a given moment, be simultaneously playing Vittoria with one of the twins while the other twin would be acting with imaginary partners. (It is relatively simple to "block" or arrange the movements of the scene so that the actors are in exactly the same positions at the end as they were at the beginning, allowing the scene to be acted as an "endless loop.") As in certain of the other sections, the length of this image may be indeterminate, ending on a prearranged signal according to the "feel" of the particular audience and performance.

9.   (*Perhaps this section is performed without a blackout after the preceding section. All of the previously used projections may be repeated during this image. At first they are merely flashed on and off quickly at any point on or around the stage. They move in unpredictable ways, their number and frequency increases, they scatter through the whole auditorium, and they remain on for increasingly long durations.*)

All of the actors perform independently, following the same rules of behavior. Each says a line or phrase from the basic scene, walks two or three steps, stops, and remains motionless for a few seconds, then repeats the procedure, walking in a different direction. At first the speeches are merely mimed with no sound being uttered. Then individual words and fragments of phrases are heard. Gradually the frequency of voiced speech and the lengths of the statements increase. As the image develops, actors move randomly down from the stage and toward the audience, leaving the auditorium independently by whatever doors are available when the section reaches its climax.

At about the same time that I was doing *Expo Alogical*, Marta Minujin said that she was negotiating with an educational television station about an avant-garde performance program and asked me for a script she could submit to them. Since there were other artists involved in the project, my script may not be the reason that it never was produced. At any rate, I still like the script. It is interesting to think about the type of image that can be presented only on television (or in a film). That is one of the things that this script is "about."

A TELEVISION PRESENTATION

NOTES: *1*) A battery or "wall" of, say, nine or twelve television sets should be set up. About ten seconds after the program begins, a tape of it is screened on the first set; ten seconds later, the program begins on the second set; and so forth. Thus nine sets would, at any moment, show a "memory" of the preceding ninety seconds of the program broken into ten-second intervals. A picture of this "memory wall" would then be broadcast at the beginning of the piece and during divisions between sections for whatever duration was necessary.

If this is not practical, brief sections of black, numbers, and/or sequential emblematic still photographs may separate the sections.

2) Except during the section with the tape recorders, all speech betwen the director and the cameramen, etc. is broadcast. There is no other sound or musical accompaniment.

3) The single performer could be of either sex. I have indicated a girl.

1. Medium shot of studio floor. No performers in sight. Markings on floor: taped lines and numbers indicating television cameras, their positions and movements. A white box or stand in the center with a diagram on it.

Dolly in to closeup of diagram. It is the same as studio floor: a map of camera placements, etc.

Hands reach into frame, placing scale model television cameras in their positions on the map.

Dolly back to medium long shot of studio. Cameras are now in the positions that are marked on the floor . . . just as the corresponding model cameras are now on the map.

Closed-circuit television rear-projected on "back" wall shows (huge) closeup of performer's hand as she moves model of camera.

2. Medium shot: three or four tape recorders. Performer behind first with a microphone. The same tape runs through all the machines in a loop. The first machine is on "record," the others on "play."

Closeup: performer counting into microphone.

Medium shot: performer counting, rear projection screen in the background. Closeup of face counting, right profile, appears on right half of rear-projection screen. Closeup of face counting, left profile, appears on left half of rear-projection screen.

Long shot: performer, machines, and rear-projection screen with two closeups. As tape moves through machines two, three, and four, the performer's voice is "echoed" several times. She counts at a two- to three-second interval, and there are intervals (distances) of about four, six, and eight seconds between machines. As she continues to record, the "echoes" are rerecorded along with her voice, and the density builds until the starting point of the tape again reaches the first machine.

3. Long shot: the rear-projection wall from straight front; the performer at one side. Perhaps beginning in leotards, she begins to put on a uniform: coat, shoes, gloves, hat, and so forth. After about six seconds, a television tape of her movements is projected life-size on the screen. (That is, the tape is delayed about six seconds and runs continuously through the remainder of the section.) About six seconds later, the "memory" image moves on the screen: now two "memories," of six and twelve seconds ago, can be seen, along with the live performer. At regular intervals, an additional "memory" image is

added to the screen, each one corresponding, for clarity, to the addition of one article of clothing. (As in memory, the images get slightly dimmer as they get older.) When the screen is full (perhaps eight or nine images), the girl begins to remove the items of clothing, then stands motionless. When all of the "memory" images are motionless, the section is over.

4. Medium-long shot: the rear-projection wall from straight front. Three rectangles of light, side by side, appear at regular intervals on the screen. They are on for five seconds, dark for two seconds, and so forth. Each rectangle may be either (a) a slide, (b) a motion picture, (c) white light in which the live performer stands. Only one action is used (although the sequence could be enlarged by adding one or more actions): the performer kneels, picks up a Polaroid camera from the floor, aims it and lowers it. The particular arrangement of the image is:

	Left Rectangle	*Center Rectangle*	*Right Rectangle*
1)	slide (front view)	slide (front view)	slide (front view)
2)	slide (left side)	slide (front view)	slide (right side)
3)	slide (front view)	motion picture (front view)	slide (front view)
4)	slide (left side)	motion picture (front view)	slide (right side)
5)	slide (negative, front view)	live performer (front view)	slide (negative, front view)
6)	slide (negative, left side)	live performer (front view)	slide (negative, right side)
7)	slide (front view)	motion picture (front view)	live performer (front view)

	Left Rectangle	*Center Rectangle*	*Right Rectangle*
8)	live performer (front view)	motion picture (front view)	slide (front view)
9)	motion picture (slow motion)	motion picture (normal speed)	motion picture (fast speed)
10)	same, negative	same, negative	same, negative
11)	motion picture (left side)	live performer (front view)	motion picture (right side)
12)	same	same	same
13)	motion picture (front view)	live performer (front view)	motion picture (front view)
14)	same	same	same
15)	same	same	same
16)	slide (front view)	live performer (frozen front view)	slide (front view)

(Number 16 remains on for ten seconds.)

5.   (*In this section, unless otherwise indicated, four television pictures are combined in broadcast so that each takes up one-quarter of the screen. These are produced by four cameras set at the corners of an imaginary square. All four are aimed toward the center where the performer stands at a table with a wire rack on it.*)

Four closeups of performer's face. She slowly lowers and raises her head; turns completely around.

Four extreme closeups of portions (quarters) of the performer's face, arranged so that the face is complete. The cameras slowly move partially around the performer and back again, so that the "complete" face becomes "disassembled" and "assembled" again.

Four extreme closeups of portions (quarters) of the performer's face, arranged so that the face is complete. Each camera in turn zooms in and then back, so that the "complete" face becomes disassembled and reassembled.

Single long shot by camera #1. It pans from the camera on its left (camera #2) to the one on its right (camera #4). In the center, probably visible all the time, is the performer and, behind her, camera #3.

This single pan shot is repeated by each of the cameras in turn. (During the preceding shot, the performer kneels, picks up a Polaroid camera from the floor, takes a photograph of camera #1, and develops it. She photographs each television camera in turn and develops the photographs.)

Four simultaneous long-shots of the business in the center. (Polaroid photographing is still going on.)

Four-shot: camera #1 moves to medium shot followed in turn, at regular intervals, by each of the others. Performer has now completed the polaroid photographs and is placing each one in the wire rack so that each television camera is faced by a photograph of itself.

Four-shot: all cameras slowly zoom in to extreme closeups of the polaroid photographs.

6.   Extreme closeup of the inside of a white box—a model or miniature stage. Identical positive and negative slides of the studio, cameras, performer, and so forth, are simultaneously projected on the white surfaces and slowly brought together so that they are superimposed. The performer's hands reach in and place or move small mirrors so that portions of the projected images are "cut out" and reflected to other spots on the walls of the box.

Positive and negative films of the studio, preceding images from the program, and so forth, are projected into the box. The performer continues to redirect segments of them with small mirrors.

The camera pulls back to a long-shot showing the performer at the small box stage, while behind her a huge closeup of the box fills the rear projection screen.

-- D E S T R U C T I O N   I N   A R T ,   I I

After the presentations in the rear yard of Judson Memorial Church, the Destruction in Art evening moved indoors for a symposium. The panelists sat at a long table facing the over-flow crowd that filled the folding chairs and stood at the sides and rear of the room. Before the discussion began, Charlotte Moorman was to perform a piece by Nam June Paik. Gripping a violin by its neck, she held it straight out in front of her and began raising it very slowly. I had seen Paik do the piece several years before, but it was obvious to everyone that she would eventually smash the violin on the table in front of her. The spectators, a number of whom had been quite noisy all evening, began to shout comments. One man stood up, walked some-what hesitantly to the table, and gestured to Charlotte to stop. She glared at him: "How dare you! Go and sit down!" He did, and she began the piece again.

Then Saul Gottlieb moved to the table. Just as I had fol-lowed John Wilcock's lead in saving the chicken, Saul thought that the man who had tried to stop Charlotte had had the right idea. He lay down on the table so that she would not have a hard surface on which to smash the violin, and began trying to justify his actions to the spectators, who were, of course, taking sides. It was awkward to lie there and also talk to the audience; Saul got up again and sat in front of Charlotte, trying to debate with the more vocal spectators and also watch what was being done behind him with the violin. Charlotte was very upset. The other members of the panel watched helplessly, obviously un-willing to use force and apparently not even interested in persuasion. As I saw it, Charlotte was torn between doing the work as it should be done by slowly raising the violin and completing the piece by breaking the instrument: she raised it hesitantly but quickly, aiming, I thought, for the table beside Saul. A spectator warned Saul. He had half-turned when Charlotte hit him with the violin. She struck him several times on the head and upraised arm, smashing the violin.

Saul Gottlieb was bleeding. He stood dabbing at his temple with a handkerchief. Everyone seemed stunned. Charlotte was apologetic and tried to help. And I wondered about why I felt Saul had been so wrong in what he had tried to do. Of course, Charlotte was wrong, too, but that was a more obvious matter. I remembered Saul yelling in answer to a spectator, " 'All art is politics'—Aristotle." I did not agree with that at all, but in political terms it seemed like a fascistic act to tell a person she could not perform a certain piece. Prohibition of art could not be justified on any grounds; you cannot tell someone he cannot do something merely because you dislike it or do not agree with it. And I remembered how, by freeing the chicken just a little while before, I had prevented Ralph Ortiz from doing the piece that he had planned. Maybe, as the censorship people like to think, art *can* be immoral, at least at some ultimate point. Or perhaps the difference between art and life has really been eliminated—a goal some artists say they are trying to accomplish—and I am not yet aware of it.

Embedded
Sculpture

In 1965 I did the first piece of what I have come to call my "embedded" sculpture. The living room of my loft was illuminated, in part, by two metal-shaded bulbs that hung from the eleven-foot ceiling. I merely bought an identical connecting box, cord, socket, shade and bulb, which I assembled, hung from the ceiling conduit, and painted entirely white to match the color of the room. This gave me an entirely non-functional "ghost light" that echoed its two functional counterparts.

All of my older sculpture was stored away in the studio. When visitors asked what kind of work I did, I pointed to the "ghost light." They were not very much impressed. If I did not point it out, no one noticed it. Even with the bulb painted white, they apparently assumed it was a functional unit. But the piece gave me a lot of pleasure. I liked its invisibility and the way it structured the natural space of the room. The two ordinary lights were really part of the piece. It was like a hypnotic melody of three notes. If the white unit were taken out of the room and hung somewhere else, it would be pointless and "nonexistent." Its aesthetic content depended upon its relationship to the particular things around it. It was "embedded" in its immediate environment.

At the same time, I began working on other embedded works, some of which I thought of as "paintings" because they hung on the wall. One was merely a rectangular white surface with a rigid sheet of transparent plastic jutting out into the room at an angle from the left edge. Looking through the plastic toward the white surface, I could also see the reflection of the window, plants, table, and other environmental details to my left. Closing one eye and keeping my head in one position, I "copied" the reflection as I looked through it, drawing in pencil on the white surface. Again the piece was almost invisible. You had to stand quite close to see the drawing, but I liked the way the plastic mediated between the reversed picture and the real things the picture represented, making a "translation field" between the two. And I liked the way the arrangement of the three-dimensional element protruding into the room was determined not by my taste but by the functional angle that was necessary to "project" a reflection onto the white rectangle.

Another wall piece was embedded by referring to the shower heads in the automatic sprinkler system that protected the loft. In the piece an identical sprinkler head, painted white, jutted out from the left side of a white rectangular field; sunlight coming in the window at the left would cast a shadow on the blank white surface. At the bottom of the piece three truncated rectangular prism protrusions aimed their slanting front faces at the shower heads capping each of the three pipes that were suspended near the ceiling. Each aimed face contained the mirror drawing of the sprinkler head toward which it was directed. (To get these drawings, I placed a thin plastic sheet over a small mirror reflecting the sprinkler head, drew the reflection on the plastic, and then transferred it in ink to drawing board.) Thus in this piece, objects that were quite far away were brought close in replica where they could be seen in detail, and mental structure was created by the cognitive "lines" joining the real sprinkler heads to their drawn "reflections" on the piece.

The mental structure, which was not tangible but seemed very real to me, was not apparent or visible to everyone. I still remember watching my sister-in-law as she looked at the piece for the first time. She was not particularly informed about modern art, and I had not discussed the new work with her at all, but I saw her turn to look up at the real sprinkler heads, mentally connecting them to the piece before she commented on the relationship. But I have also watched several more artistically sophisticated people who did not really see the piece because they were not considering the specific relationship to things around it. If a person does not look at the environmental elements that are really part of the piece, he has not seen my work. And in this case, one can tell something of what a person sees, or does not see, by watching him.

Another of the early wall pieces was my first use of photography. It was a simple piece that sandwiched a positive transparency of a photograph between a mirror and a protective front sheet of glass. The photograph printed in the large transparency was the same view of the room that was reflected in the mirror. One could look through the transparent photograph and compare it with the reflection. Of course, the real reflection changed with the viewer's distance and angle, but the relationship with the static photo always existed. One of the things that I liked about this piece was the way time was involved. A photograph fixes and preserves a moment of time; changes in the room reflected in the mirror made it clear that, in addition to the purely spatial comparisons involved, it was that past moment that was being compared to the present.

All of my sculpture since the early mirror piece has used

photographs in one way or another. There are two general possibilities: The photograph may depict what would be seen in a mirror if a mirror were placed in that position in the piece, or it may show what would be seen if you could see through the surface on which the photograph is mounted or through the opening it fills. The first possibility could be illustrated by a large rectangular plywood box or broad column that stood near the center of the room. One half of the top portion was the negative imprint of the patterned tin molding and ceiling in the corresponding corner of the room, and the other half of the top, which was cut away at the appropriate angle, held a large negative mirror-photograph of the opposite corner. An early example of the second photographic possibility was a large box without top or bottom that was raised off the floor on a branching central base. The outside faces of the box were blank, but looking down into it one could see enlarged photographic views of the four corresponding walls of the room.

In 1966 I began to work in metal. Mounted photographs could be inserted into the framework of square and rectangular tubing and rods of which the pieces were built. For one thing, I wanted work that could be exhibited in a gallery and sold. The earlier pieces were so absolutely embedded in the place for which they were conceived that, although they could be physically moved quite easily, it was pointless to view them in any other place. They could not even be moved to different spots in my living room; each had its own exact place. Of course, replicas or modified versions of the earlier pieces could have been built for anyone who wanted one, but in the newer pieces, it was only a matter of taking new photographs and substituting them for the photographs that embedded the piece in my home. I used aluminum because it was easy to work with and relatively inexpensive; bronze was used when a color contrast was needed. Metal, particularly bronze, is a traditional sculptural material, and I wanted to refer to the tradition—to put my work in a more traditionally sculptural context—by using it.

Since the earlier work, my embedded sculptures have grown larger and more complicated. One of the largest metal pieces is basically an arrangement of four regular truncated pyramids that hold photographs in both bases and have matte aluminum sides. I think of a truncated pyramid as having spatial direction, as *aiming* from the large base toward the smaller one. In this piece, one of the pyramids aims straight up toward the ceiling, raised off the floor on tubular legs; a mirror on the floor within the framework of the legs allows a person to see the photograph in the large end of the pyramid by reflection without bending over. A second pyramid is joined to the first, their small bases forming a forty-five-degree angle to the first. The sixteen-inch square enlargements mounted in the large base of each pyramid are photographs taken through the hollow pyramid, showing that portion of the environment toward which it is aimed; in the smaller bases are reversed or "mirror" negative prints of the large photos. Thus these three directional boxes "'cut through" the space in a single vertical plane that extends from vertical to horizontal. Suspended at the end of horizontal extensions, the fourth truncated prism aims back at the others; they can be seen in the photograph in its large base. In the negative version of this photograph that fills the small inner base, the negative photos in the other pyramids can be seen as positive: one negative reverses another. The piece is reflexive. In addition to looking at the space of the room in a particular way, it looks back on itself.

If the two functional lights were considered as parts of the original "ghost light" piece, it could be thought of as being in three separate, detached parts. But more recently I have constructed "single" pieces in more than one part: sections of the same piece have been spatially discrete. For example, a unit of one of the pieces is a wedge-shaped framework of square aluminum tubing. Photographs taken from each side, showing the recession in perspective of the aluminum bars and the environment beyond, are mounted in the openings so that one can "look through" the framework only in the photographs.

Copies of these same photographs, which include the metal structure, are then mounted to make an identical wedge-shaped solid that exists only in photographs. This entirely photographic section, a "memory" of the first, so to speak, is placed in another part of the room, in a different room, or even a different country. There it is backed with a bronze structure identical to the original aluminum one; joined together the two wedges made a diamond-shaped solid. The photographic procedure is repeated with the bronze unit, forming another entirely photographic "memory" that completes the original aluminum section. Thus each of the two diamond-shaped sections, which could theoretically be thousands of miles away from each other, is photographically embedded in its own environment and also contains a record of the other unit and the environment it is in. Other pieces "transmit" photographic views from one section to another through space in analogous ways.

In all of these embedded sculptures I am concerned, as I mentioned earlier, with the permeation of space by an ideational structure. The fact that the extensive shape of the piece is intangible and exists, in a sense, only in the mind of the spectator does not make it less real than the tangible material of paper photographs, metal, and wood. The physical structure of a piece exists primarily to generate the ideational structure; it is not conceived as a visual entity in itself.

Since it is not the retinal configuration or image that is of major importance, one cannot see this work at a glance. Only through time can the complete mental shape be known. This is not necessarily a problem. Any traditional sculpture that depends for its apprehension on the subjective assembly of a connected sequence of views does somewhat the same thing: It takes time before the whole piece can be seen. I am attempting in this way to create work that is psychically, rather than physically, dynamic. The mental process of ascertaining the true shape of the piece is the dynamic aspect. And since this shape is intangible, it remains more "alive" and less easy to focus than does static physical mass.

Nor are the particular images in the photographs of any particular significance. The content, details, and composition of the photographs usually depend entirely on the placement of the piece rather than on standards of visual taste: A particular position makes very exact demands as to what is included in the photographs. The embedded pieces "look at" whatever is there to be seen. There are occasional exceptions to this general rule, because some pieces are designed to look at certain specific things. One piece, for example, can only be placed in that exact spot where the four corners of one wall of a room are "reflected" in the mirror-photographs of its four slanting faces. Even in these cases, however, the imagery does not *mean* anything: it does not matter in terms of information. The work, therefore, is completely abstract, although it involves imagery. This may sound like a contradiction, but in any except the most superficial sense it is true, giving the work a unique character.

_____ POLITICS

When I was doing *The First and Second Wilderness,* I was told that Jackson MacLow and Dick Higgins were threatening to picket the performance. I do not think I had met either one at the time. When I asked why they would do a thing like that, the answer was "misuse of the chance method."

Perhaps my choice of a game between players dressed as Union and Confederate soldiers as the central image in my performance had been suggested somehow by my knowledge that various people were using chance techniques in creating art, but I never consciously intended to follow their line of investigation. I do not think I knew very much then about the exact methods that Jackson, Dick, and others were using, but I certainly knew they were not interested in chance for its implications as an image of war or anything else. I could understand how they might dislike my work without even seeing it, but I could not understand how chance, or any other method, could be "misused."

The picketing never materialized. Years later when I mentioned it to Dick Higgins, he said that he had felt that "it was the wrong time to refight the Civil War." "Well," I answered, "I was just trying to find a war where it wasn't *them* against *us* —the 'bad guys' against the 'good guys.'" Of course, that was not the whole story, but World War II would not have been the same thing.

Sculpture
as a
Visual
Instrument

When some people look at Larry Bell's recent work, they see
only empty glass boxes. Perhaps they interpret them, meta-
phorically, as manifestations of West Coast Zen or, historically,
as transparent primary sculptures relating to Robert Morris'
solid boxes. Since Bell's pieces are made of tinted glass, however, they are not only transparent, but their several faces
reflect and rereflect images of the room in which they stand.
It is these transmissions and reflections of the environmental
space that, to me, constitute much of the material and, therefore, the content of the work.

    If this is true, we have been trained or habituated not to see
what Bell has done. Reflections in the framed glass protecting
a painting, drawing, or pastel are obviously not part of the

work, and we attempt to ignore the glass, minimize the reflected interference, and mentally compensate for the viewing conditions. This is never easy. It requires energy. At times it fails completely. We attempt to see Seurat's *La Grande Jatte,* for example, and are frustrated by the impenetrable reflections. (As one is forced to search for clear, unmarred details and then assemble them into an intelligible whole, the failure must be obvious to anyone trying to see the painting under the glass, but perhaps only those who saw it before it was entombed can fully appreciate the magnitude of the loss.) At any rate, defense against such interference is so often necessary that it becomes forceful and automatic.

But the fact that extraneous reflections often work against the perception of a work itself and must therefore be mentally and/or physically eliminated as much as possible does not mean that reflection may not be an intrinsic part of certain works. In Bell's work the reflections, rereflections (or reflections of reflections), and images seen through the piece are organized by the cubic arrangement of the glass into complex structures. In this sense they are much more "systemic," to use Lawrence Alloway's term for a wide range of contemporary art, than they are "primary." As the viewer moves, the movement of the images adds another dimension to this perceptually elaborate system created by a relatively simple construction. It is not the relationships or qualities of the box itself which are of primary importance, but the qualities and structure of the images seen *by means of the work.* These constitute much of its basic aesthetic material: the work is an *instrument* for seeing rather than merely an object.

(There is little doubt in my mind that these effects are not part of Bell's conscious intent. I am told that a few years ago he was so opposed to the reflections and transmissions that he felt the ideal way to exhibit a box would be in an empty white room with the viewer looking through an aperture of some sort so that he was not reflected. I can only discuss the work as I have seen it, however, and the question I prefer to consider is not whether an artist achieves or fails to achieve what he thinks and says he is attempting but what type of experience his work causes. If I find great interest and implications in Bell's work for what, I am sure, are the "wrong" reasons, I cannot deny that experience because of any teleological concerns. At the same time, a certain unconscious intent might be deduced from the relationship of the present transparent boxes to his earlier mirror boxes, in which images from the "outside world" entered the pieces through clear oval "windows" in the mirror walls and were reflected internally in various configurations. It should also be pointed out that the present boxes, while "all alike" to some observers, vary in size and the color or tint of the glass used: these seemingly minor variations produce comparatively great changes in the amount, size, or scale of the reflected images, and change the hues of both transmitted and reflected images to a significant degree.)

Webster's dictionary defines "instrument" as "a tool or implement, especially one used for delicate work or for scientific or artistic purposes" and as "a thing by means of which something is done." The "something" which Bell's boxes "do" is the combination and arrangement of visual images from the environment. The use of the box by the spectator, involving movement and choice as it does, is more physical and active, than, say, reading a painting. And in this case it happens to be "delicate work."

In considering works of art which are, in this sense, "instruments," I should like to focus only on those which, like Bell's boxes, may be considered visual or visual-mental instruments. Some pieces which can be "used," like Joseph Cornell's *Forgotten Game,* into which the viewer drops a small ball and watches its progress as it rolls down past rows of small windows or, more to the point, his various boxes of layered glass in which sand and free objects may be infinitely rearranged by tilting the box, may be thought of as *physical* instruments. Marta Minujin's *Minuphone,* oriented as it is toward a diversity of media, is a more recent example of physical "instrumentation": the spectator *uses* the telephone in the booth to make an actual phone call, his voice is distorted, his image appears on a television screen under his feet, he causes wind and shadow effects, etc. But without the physical participation of the observer, the piece does not exist. Although these examples may suggest what I mean by "instrument" in a more graphic and forceful way, I am concerned here only with visual and visual-mental use. ("Visual-mental" refers to the comprehension of relationships and structures which are not entirely retinal but are directly deduced or inferred from visual data.)

Although this is only one element in a subtle and complex work, *The Bride Stripped Bare by Her Bachelors, Even*, combines what is seen through the glass with what is reflected in it: if the spectator moves, which he naturally does, these dual "pictures" move as they relate to the static images that Duchamp placed on the glass. This use of transmitted and reflected images is not truly "instrumental" in that Duchamp is concerned with bringing environmental imagery into the work to serve as a shifting contextural field rather than with a way of looking at the surrounding space, but his simple simultaneous comparison between the space behind the plane of the glass and the space in front of it is basic to the vocabulary of pieces, such as Bell's, which refer to real space in a more elaborate and essential way.

Like Duchamp's *Large Glass*, Pistoletto's paintings on highly polished steel compare reflections with painted images, but the realistic subject matter and natural scale in the latter's work make it more clearly instrumental. The spectator, through his own movement, may move the reflected background of the painted people and may enter into the picture himself if he chooses.

In Charles Ross's *Islands of Prisms*, shown last May and June in the 1967 *Schemata 7* exhibit at the Finch College Museum, triangular prisms made of clear plastic in various lengths and filled with colorless mineral oil were hung in groups with the upper face parallel to the floor at chest height. Each group or "island" made up a horizontal, regular, rectangular grid in space: the spaces between the prisms in each group equaled the width of the prisms. Looking down at one of these grids, the viewer was presented alternately with the images within the prisms and an equal "slice" of the floor and space beneath the piece. A prism, unlike a sheet of glass which has parallel faces, bends the light passing through it, and, being triangular with two of the three faces slanting at a sixty-degree angle to the floor, these prisms "picked up" and transmitted images from unexpected parts of the room. In the longest groups, the same image—perhaps another spectator or the observer's own foot—appeared in two or more prisms and, although broken by an equally coherent grid of the "real" environment, could be read as a whole. In the smaller prisms, the refracted images were so truncated that they were unrecognizable, appearing only as shapes and colors.

Color is important in Ross's work. In refraction, different wave lengths of light are bent unequally, causing the hues to separate, as in a rainbow, and Ross increases this effect by using mineral oil, which has greater density, and therefore, greater refractive power, than water or air. The image of a spotlight, for example, seen "in" the work takes on a color or colors it does not "actually" have; an object is surrounded by a multicolored glow or aureole. Although identical in linear detail to the environment, the world "within" the prisms has its own chromaticity.

(With Ross there is no doubt about his conscious intent to do instrumental work: in an interview published in the catalogue for the *Schemata 7* show, he said, "When you look at one of the prisms, you see the form of the piece, you see into it and you see through it, all simultaneously. . . . This puts you in touch with the space you are in in several different ways. When you are walking toward them and the floor turns into the ceiling, you experience a spatial shift in your own reading of the gallery.")

In my own work, although clear glass and mirrors are sometimes used, the primary elements are photographs of the space in which the piece is placed. For example, the *Window Piece,* which was in the *Schemata 7* exhibition, contained, among other elements, a central square made of aluminum tubing;

two similar bars of metal joining the four corners divided the interior of the square into four equal triangles. In one of the triangles a mirror was mounted so that it was slightly above eye level: the viewer did not see himself included in the reflection of the upper parts of the room. In the next triangle was a "mirror-photograph"—a photograph showing what would be reflected if a mirror filled the space. The other two triangles contained, respectively, clear glass through which one looked out the window and a photograph of the exterior view (the fire escape, trees, the neighboring apartment building) that one would see if the space were empty or also held clear glass. Thus the central portion of the piece set up several comparisons involving interior and exterior space, distance, fixed images (the photographs), and changeable images (the mirror and clear glass). In this case the visual-mental structure consisted basically of a horizontal axis joining space behind the observer with space at some distance in front of him. Although the piece was physically two-dimensional, this intangible—but no less real—aspect made it essentially three-dimensional.

To a greater or lesser degree it would seem that the images and image systems "in" each of the visual instruments that have been mentioned should also be compared, as part of the aesthetic experience, with their "real" counterparts and related elements in the environment. This, of course, requires an entirely different perceptual attitude from those that are traditionally used with sculpture. Just as our minds have learned to compensate for the interference of the glass in front of a painting and to eliminate whatever extraneous perceptual data are received from it, we have had, in most cases, years of practice in ignoring the surrounding environment—the wall on which a picture hangs; what can be seen beyond and around a piece of sculpture—so that we can perceive the work itself as completely and accurately as possible. When art becomes a visual instrument, however, the opposite "set" becomes necessary, and awareness must clearly include the real space from which images are taken and to which references are being made. Such a mental state is quite different from that which is called for by the total emphasis on physicality in the main stream of contemporary sculpture.

This necessary change in perceptual attitude does not mean, however, that these pieces are not sculpture. Most of the examples given stand in the same physical relationship to the observer as traditional sculpture does. Although they make environmental reference, they are not Environments. Unlike Kusama's and Samaras' mirror rooms, for example, they do not enclose the observer. Any spatial structure which surrounds the viewer is not tangible but visual-mental.

Indeed, the fact that these constructions have a physical shape and mass in space which is definitely sculptural in the traditional sense is an important aspect of the work. Just as instruments such as the telephone and the microscope coexist with the sounds and images which are their intangible aspects, this concrete three-dimensionality exists simultaneously with, and in relation to, the visual-mental structure which is also three-dimensional. In some cases the physical structure is entirely determined or generated by the surrounding nonphysical structure, while in other cases, such as Bell's boxes, there is an equal balance between the two. If the concrete takes precedence over the visual-mental structure, the work is not, in my terminology, an "instrument." Not every piece which involves reflections, for example, uses them instrumentally. Reflections of environmental space are a quality of any highly polished work—Von Schleegal's metal constructions, among many others. At other times, as in *The Large Glass*, environmental material may be incorporated as an element. But the differences between quality or isolated element and visual-mental system are great, and only when the nonphysical structure of environmental reference is as clear and elaborate as the physical structure does the piece take on the character of "instrument."

In conclusion, we may say that the description of a piece of sculpture as a visual instrument does not depend upon specific formal, material, or stylistic aspects of the work, but upon the particular state of mind involved in its perception. While demonstrating significant technical and structural diversity, all of the examples noted here make use of imagery—either "living" moving images taken by direct transmission, reflection, or refraction from the surrounding environment itself, or static photographs of that environment—and all, in contrast to the majority of sculptures which could be called physical instruments, tend to be contemplative and essentially intimate. These are not necessarily defining factors, however, and the most important consideration is how sculpture as a visual instrument requires the observer to use an entirely different mode of perception from that which is fitting for traditional sculpture.

--- IN ROOM 706

After polaroid photographs of the three audience sections had been projected, the final part of *Room 706* was the prerecorded sound of applause. For some unknown reasons, the tape recorder would not play. Perhaps it would have started, but I walked out to where Tom Downes was working over the machine, announced to the audience that they were supposed to be hearing applause from the tape, and indicated that the piece was over. Naturally, the spectators applauded. In a moment, as everyone stood and prepared to leave, Tom got the machine working, and the recorded applause could be heard.

Although I had not advertised the performances, the "grapevine" had passed the word, and Oscar Masotta, whom I had never met, attended. After he returned to Argentina, he edited and wrote a book on Happenings (called, unsurprisingly, *Happenings*) in which he described the performance. As he remembered it, I had announced that the spectators were to hear "their own voices . . . in the same way they had seen the photographs" of themselves. He described the applause, then wrote, "We had just begun to leave when we heard the treacherous clamor of our own applause—which Kirby had carefully recorded—accompanying our steps."

Perhaps Masotta improved on the piece. His version is more in keeping with the general development of the images than mine had been. He certainly gave me more credit than I deserved. At any rate, accidents in performance are sometimes beneficial and are frequently not recognized as accidents. (Or it may only be that I have misunderstood Masotta's Spanish just as he "misunderstood" the end of my presentation.)

Marjorie Strider's
Interdimensional
Sculpture

In January, 1964, Marjorie Strider showed a huge *Tryptych* in the First International Girlie Exhibition at the Pace Gallery in New York. Lichtenstein, Warhol, and Wesselman were among those represented by paintings of girls. It was at the height of Pop Art. But even though the subject matter, the bold size, and the use of flat unmodulated color and severely limited palette were characteristics definitely relating Strider's tryptych to Pop Art, there was a formal concern in the piece that indicated the direction her work was to take in the succeeding years. A study of Strider's recent development not only illustrates her personal transfiguration of Pop into a different figurative idiom but, more importantly, demonstrates a new answer to one of the key questions or problems of modern art.

235

The tryptych that was part of the First International Girlie Exhibition shows the same brunette girl in a bathing suit in each of the three separately hung paintings. "Reading" from left to right, one could receive the impression that the larger-than-life-sized girl had moved—raising both hands behind her head in the center panel, dropping one arm and leaning back slightly in the last painting. The particular pose and movement emphasized the bust, and, rather than being merely painted, the breasts in each panel were built out three-dimensionally from the flat background. These two concerns, motion and the combination of sculptural and pictorial dimensionality, were to remain central to Strider's work.

The pieces in her first one-man show at the Pace Gallery in January, 1965, most of which focused on flower or vegetable subject matter, all employed a smooth transition from "flat," two-dimensional, represented space to "real," three-dimensional, sculptural form. A small tryptych, *Columbine,* for example, consisted of a painting of the flower in the first panel, a second "picture" in which sculptured petals joined with painted ones in approximately equal balance, and a final panel in which the entire flower projected physically from the flat ground. (In terms of movement, there was a signified "growth" into the space of the room.) Other works, such as *Diagonal Red* that suspended a gigantic and completely three-dimensional tomato on a hidden rear support in front of a half-round and half-painted tomato, combined the movement from two to three dimensions in relation to a single rectangle. Because the plastic steps in these progressions were equally spaced and a consistent use of color unified the painted projections and their grounds, a certain illusionistic ambivalence was achieved even when the essentially frontal works were seen from an angle. I remember the shocked reaction of a woman when she suddenly realized that a Strider "painting" hanging in front of her in the living room where she had been sitting for some time was not entirely flat as she had assumed from its traditional rectangular format. In these earlier works, the sculptural was used to heighten the "presence" of the pictorial, but sculpture and represented volume retained their own integrities while being smoothly blended together.

A key work in the January, 1965, exhibition was *Open Space,* now in Buffalo's Albright-Knox Museum, the only piece that did not hang on the walls of the gallery. A series of huge, light yellow and blue, completely three-dimensional blossoms rose from a low base and were "enclosed" within an essentially two-dimensional gold picture frame. The frame established a frontality that was not inherent in the basic plastic grouping of blossoms, which could be viewed equally well from any position. Or, rather, two frontalities were created for the omnidirectional central mass, since the sculpture was converted into a "painting" by viewing it from either side of the frame. In this piece the equally balanced coexistence of dimensionalities that characterized Strider's earlier work was presented in a somewhat different way, but the equation remained undisturbed. Each partner in the union kept its own integrity in these pieces, but the balance was about to be broken. Both painting and sculpture were to "lose" some autonomy as their relationship within her work became more "difficult" and complex.

In Strider's show of December, 1965, at the Pace Gallery, two-dimensional "illusion" and three-dimensional "reality" were no longer compatible, although they continued to live together. In *Double Bean,* as in the unexhibited *Double Day Lily* and other works of the same year, the sculptural shape and the painted vision disputed for supremacy without a winner. A monochrome plastic relief was partly overlapped by a multi-colored painting of the same subject. If viewed from a direct frontal position, the two-dimensional picture could be seen as complete, but because it overlapped the sculpture, a change in viewing angle brought increasing disruption and discontinuity to the pictorial image. On the other hand, the boldness and strength of the colors used in the painting tended to "destroy" the sculpture at the points where they fused and to interfere with the understanding of the masses and their contours.

In these pieces there was "conflict" without a "victor"—a fact that, of course, explains rather than detracts from the aesthetic success of the work—but two large pieces that were focal points of the December show indicated interesting directions that the deepening "dispute" was to take. In *View From a Window III,* sculpture dominated the illusionism of painting. The two-dimensional representation of a window, the sill and frame done in linear perspective, was "projected" from two sides onto two huge sculptured clouds that hung from the ceiling. From opposite sides of the clouds, facing their long axis, the picture of the window completed itself even across the empty space between the two separate bulbous masses that touched each other at only one point: The lines of the window appeared to be straight. But from most of the possible viewing angles, the lines appeared curved as they followed the curved surfaces upon which they were painted, and they made no "sense" representationally. (Abstractly, they were a striking visual system that owed its integrity not to composition, balance, and subjective adjustment in the traditional manner but to the governing illusionistic premise upon which it was based. Although quite different in style, it may, in this sense, be compared to certain systemic works, such as Sol LeWitt's recent serial pieces, in which the presented form depends on preconceived and objective rules rather than on "internal" subjective adjustments.) While the plastic clouds retained their identity from any point of view, it was possible for an observer to "misunderstand" the painting and to be unaware of the representational reference involved in it. Thus sculpture, in this piece, could be seen as "defeating" picture-plane painting.

According to a general preference in our time for the "real" and substantive over the "illusionistic" and pictorial, this outcome might seem the only possible one. But in Marjorie Strider's *View From a Window II,* exhibited in the same show, the first signs of the victory that painting was later to win in her work could be seen. A moon, also suspended from the ceiling by almost invisible nylon cord, was "wrapped" by a window in almost the same manner as the clouds. It was not a full moon, however, and the sphere was sliced away in a slightly curved plane at one side. The "picture" of a three-quarter moon had destroyed the substance of the moon itself. That part of the moon that was hidden in shadow did not exist—perhaps an optical truth on a dark night, but hardly a physical one. Two-dimensional representation had "overcome" sculpture in this work, imposing its principles on the three-dimensional mass and leaving a concave truncation that was inconsistent with the plastic representation.

(Although movement was not primary in these pieces, the color in *Double Bean,* for example, could be seen as "sliding off" the pod and its contents to which it was at one time fixed, and the moon and clouds embodied subjects that moved, changed, and passed through phases. The facts that these latter pieces hung from the ceiling and that completeness of the thing seen was in no way interrupted or prohibited by the "walls" around the window painted on them gave a certain sense of floating passage.)

I have described Marjorie Strider's early work as involving, at first, an equal balance between two ways of representing objective phenomena and, later, as a "conflict" between these representational modes in which one or the other gained a "victory," in order to clarify the unusual qualities in her more recent work. Where the earlier work seemed to be clearly two-dimensional and three-dimensional, some of her recent pieces achieve an uncommon fusion of dimensionality, so that they seem to be neither two-dimensional nor three-dimensional in the usual sense but to exist *between* dimensions. Technically, of course, the work is sculpture, but the way that the eye sees this painted sculpture depends as much upon spatial cues related to illusionistic painting as on the "real" plastic cues.

In *Sea Surface III* (1968) this fusion is caused by the complete and consistent imposition of a two-dimensional point of view upon a sculptural representation. A thin rectangular block, modeled and painted to resemble ocean waves, is suspended in a plastic box. Although one may walk around the box and view it from all sides—it is only twenty-eight inches long, twenty-one inches wide, and five inches tall— Strider shaped and painted the waves using a photograph for reference, and they are only "correct" from a high "front" angle. From this vantage point the painted highlights and shadows help to convey the impression of deep recession, but this illusion is contradicted when the piece is seen from directly above or from the sides or rear. The pictorial space is much deeper than the sculptural space. The sculptured waves are proportionately much closer together than actual waves would be, they rise much more steeply, and they crest to a point rather than rolling forward. Unlike the moon in *View From a Window II*, the mass of which was "deformed" according to two-dimensional rules in only one place, the modeling of the waves uniformly depends upon non-sculptural determinants, while the blues and greens of the painting cause even the most extreme compressions to retain their reference to the ocean. Painting has been forced upon, and controls, sculpture.

In a like manner, the waves in *Piece of Sea II*, a vaguely rectangular block whose sloping upper modeled surface is deeper than it is wide, seem unnaturally compressed except when seen "pictorially" from a slightly elevated frontal position. In addition, they tend to be physically smaller toward the highest part, which becomes the rear as the frontality of the piece is determined. And the small "white caps" of foam that line some of the waves in the front portion do not appear toward the rear: They are "out of sight." In this piece, too, Strider worked with reference to a photograph, and it is a pictorial device, but not a sculptural one, that the size of objects and the sharpness of their detail decreases as their distance from the observer increases. Atmospheric perspective, the dimming and blueing of perceived color proportionate to the amount of air separating the observer and the object, also occurs in *Piece of Sea II* as the colors become slightly duller toward the rear. But since we can actually walk around the piece, the "front" and "rear" in terms of the viewer may change, and it becomes apparent that this device, too, is optical rather than sculptural and that the sculptural shape is being controlled by two-dimensional illusionism "projected" onto the piece from a single point.

River Landscape (1968) achieves an analogous "interdimensional" position in a more complex way. The piece rests on a stand or table so that we look down at its flat, almost square face painted to resemble an aerial view of a wooded landscape cut by rivers and spotted by lakes. The green surface of forests and fields is opaque, but we can actually see down into the rivers and lakes, where real water is flowing under the surface of transparent plastic. The water has real depth, not an illusionistic one. Its volume plainly reaffirms the vertical visual axis of the piece. But the painting denies this. The scale and angle of view change from one area of the painted landscape to another: There is no way of telling which of the illusionistic cues to our distance "above" the ground are "correct." Thus the ambiguity of the three-dimensional space is heightened by placing it behind a transparent two-dimensional surface and filling it with moving water; while textural qualities, the depth effects of color contrasts, and shifts of scale and viewing angle heighten the sense of space emanating from the flat field. Again, sculpture has "given up" some of its potential, allowing a consistent synthesis and integration of two- and three-dimensions that might be described as interdimensional.

These pieces by Marjorie Strider suggest another answer to one of the basic recurrent questions in modern art—the problem of subject matter. Cubism, in its synthetic phase, became a style that could be applied to any subject. Formal relationships became important, and subject matter became arbitrary and "unnecessary." Then Surrealism again legitimized recognizable imagery by proposing the unconscious as subject matter, and Pop Art continued this impulse, adding social reference. In Strider's latest works, the choice of subject seems to depend upon how well it is able to combine the illusionistic modes of perception related both to painting and sculpture. In these terms, it is obvious that the girl in the early *Tryptych* was chosen as a comment on our society, attitudes, and taste. The three-dimensionality of her bust, which had flat lower surfaces and angular corners, was not a purely optical statement. But the moon and clouds of the *View From a Window* pieces were not Surrealistic or Pop, although the clouds were reminiscent in subject matter of Magritte. In these pieces there was no social comment nor physicalization of the unconscious—except perhaps in the "inflated" scale they shared with Oldenburg's work. They eschewed the irrational combination of disparate images found in Magritte and the Surrealists. The pieces were optically oriented. The unification of window and what is seen through it derived from a concern with the way things and art are perceived, and Strider's latest work seems to suggest that subject matter is "justified" by the completeness of fusion it allows between two- and three-dimensional ways of seeing.

Although I have been focusing attention until now on the factors in Marjorie Strider's work that relate to the perception of illusionistic sculpture and painting, there are many elements in both the painting and the plastic characteristics of her work which are non-illusionistic. Just as two- and three-dimensional illusionistic characteristics seem, in several recent pieces, to fuse with each other, any overall illusionistic intent is usually "cancelled out" by equally strong non-illusionistic elements.

Even though museums and galleries of the nineteenth century were probably as protective of their statuary as are our contemporary ones, traditional aestheticians frequently equated sculpture with the sense of touch. They were looking for clear distinctions between the arts; it would be neat and logically reassuring if each sense had its own art, and painting had obviously preempted that of sight as music had done with hearing. There may be a little truth in this overly simple notion. Psychologists have demonstrated the role of touching in developing and validating the visual system of depth perception, and one occasionally hears a friend mention his desire to touch a particular piece of sculpture. But many of Strider's pieces seem to deny this tendency, even while they encourage it with their sensuous surfaces, by isolating the representational sculptured units within boxes of transparent plastic.

More importantly, these boxes contradict the illusionism of the works and emphasize the "thingness" of the whole. They are never merely cases to set off and protect fragile objects—such as the transparent cases used by Paul Thek and, occasionally, Lucas Samaras, for example—but serve to support illusionistic elements of the sculpture. In the *Large Splash,* modeled and painted drops of water cling to and "strike" the transparent box as they "fly out" from the central sculptured splash. The boxes aid illusionism while emphasizing the objectness of the work.

Strider also employs other non-illusionistic materials to contradict and balance the illusionism of her works. *Sea Surface I* suspends a photographic silk screen of a drawing (based on a photograph of ocean waves) above real, but artificially colored, water. The drawing represents waves, seen from a somewhat elevated vantage point, as moving from the upper left background to the lower right foreground. If hung on a wall, the illusion would be "correct" in terms of the viewer's own gravity and dimensionality, but when aligned with the surface of the real water and seen from above, it loses these illusionistic correlations. Except for its green color, there is no ambiguity about the real water. It seems to exist as a reference point to which the illusionism may be referred.

In a like manner, the water in *Sea Surface I* condenses in changing patterns on the top and sides of the box; drops of liquid glycerine cling to the transparent top and sides of *Sea Surface III* and echo the sculptured spray in *Large Splash.* Sculptural illusionism is surrounded by concrete elements of equal aesthetic importance.

If sculpture is employed both illusionistically and non-illusionistically in Strider's work, so is painting. Frequently the intense colors are not actually on the surface but under a transparent polyester coating, which gives them a physical ("sculptural") depth rather than emphasizing the surface in a "painterly" way. (In *Piece of Sea II* and *Sea Surface III*, the light reflected from this shiny surface realistically suggests the reflection on actual waves, and rather than being ignored or rejected as "not belonging to the work of art" this real but transitory element is integrated into the perception of the piece.) When color is suspended in water or glycerine, as it is in several of Strider's pieces, it becomes entirely sculptural. The volume of the liquid is completely filled with an unlocalized color. Suspended in glycerine, the color takes a brilliance and luminosity that would be impossible with surface color, again seeming to contradict the power of painting. On the other hand, representational color in the work is reminiscent of that of a color photograph: It is connotative but "too colorful" to be realistic.

Marjorie Strider's creative procedure involves intuition to a high degree—a fact it would seem unnecessary to stress if it were not for the basic "ideas" involved in her work and the current plethora of rationally based art—and one is tempted to "explain" her creations by hypothesizing a fundamental dissatisfaction with both painting and sculpture. In the same way, her concern with motion seems to invite psychological interpretation because of its ambivalent position. Many of her new pieces represent moving water—waves and splashes—but they do not actually move themselves. Yet by incorporating real liquids they have the possibility or potential of movement. *Piece of Sea I* and *Piece of Sea II* do make use of moving liquid that flows down over the sculptured surface, but here the movement itself is not important. It does not change from moment to moment, is not even visible as movement under certain conditions, and acts more as a "living" coat of paint than as a kinetic element. The water moving in the rivers and lakes of *Large Landscape* is within the picture, beneath the two-dimensional plane of the painted surface. Strider may be dissatisfied with the static nature of sculpture and painting, but she will not reject these arts for the more theatrical kinetic one that develops in time.

In conclusion, Marjorie Strider's work may, from one point of view, be seen as reflecting the "battle" that has taken place in modern art between painting and sculpture, between illusionism and "thingness." More and more artists have turned from painting to sculpture—as Strider herself did. The claim that "painting is dead" is widely supported. But Strider is still a painter even while doing sculpture, and the two-dimensional vision "lives" in her work. This work suggests a new representationalism based upon the objective facts and modes of perception rather than upon expressionism in one form or another or upon the stylistic possibilities of a particular subject. It is work that accepts both the two-dimensional and the three-dimensional visions and, in fusing them, exists "interdimensionally."

The
Experience
of Kinesis

To discuss kinetic sculpture in sociopolitical terms and relate
it to the media-dominated, automated, mechanized, scientific
character of our historical moment may, in some cases, be
quite interesting, but it tells us nothing about the work as art.
By ignoring and blurring the distinctions between individual
works, it creates the kind of generic oversimplification that, in
the cases of Pop and Op, brought discomfort to many artists
and satisfaction only to the dilettante. Kinetic sculpture—in
using the term I refer to all works which involve motion,
whether the motion of light, three-dimensional elements, or
whatever—is being produced in impressive and constantly
increasing diversity, and it is much more important to analyze
and elucidate that diversity than it is to explain away important differences in order to create a new "ism."

247

The complete description of sculpture that involves motion involves many parameters, but perhaps the most important is that of time. Movement is obviously dependent upon time, and the experience of time would seem to be at the heart of any aesthetics of kinetic sculpture. If, in a very basic and fundamental way, the structure of painting is two-dimensional and the structure of sculpture is three-dimensional, the structure of kinetic sculpture is four-dimensional: it is the structuring of time. But experience of, and in, time can have a wide diversity. We can say that there are four distinct modes in the experience of kinesis. "Pure" examples of each mode exist. And the fact that they can, at times, overlap and blend one into the other does not deny their theoretical implications.

The most complicated of the four modes involves memory and expectancy and their relationship. It is possible that each moment in the perception of a work changing with time—whether it is music, drama, dance, or kinetic sculpture—becomes charged with expectations about the future nature of the work. Since these expectations are based upon the preceding experience of the piece, and since the present state and configuration are mentally compared with whatever mental traces we have retained from previous states, each moment may be described as having a particular memory/expectancy valence. The way in which a particular piece creates and assembles memories of itself and the way in which it creates, assembles, confirms or denies expectancy may be considered its memory/expectancy structure. Recognition, which is also a kind of connection made through time, is, in this context, regarded as a form of memory.

In Chryssa's *Fragment for the Gates of Times Square, 2,* one sees a dark, almost opaque plastic box. Suddenly neon calligraphy flashes on inside, clearly visible because of its brilliance. After only three seconds, the light goes out, and the piece returns to its "inert," inscrutable state for twenty-seven seconds before it lights up again. Thus two simple, disparate, motionless sculptural images are alternated in time to create a complex memory/expectancy structure. The first burst of light we see denies our impression that the piece is static and "time-less": we are surprised. But the period of illumination is much too short for us to study adequately the complex arrangement of neon in the contemplative manner we are accustomed to use with sculpture. The frustration intensifies our desire and antic-ipation. Each time the light goes on we continue our study, based on memories of the preceding "viewing periods." Each time the light goes out we ready ourselves for very pointed, accurate observation during the next illumination. As the piece is viewed over many repetitions, predictability of the durations in the fixed cycle becomes more accurate, the an-ticipatory tension becomes modified, and memory completes the perception of the briefly illuminated figure. The structure of the piece in time makes dynamic use of the memory/expectancy mode.

On the other hand, Robert Breer's work makes use of memory/expectancy in an entirely different way. While Chryssa's piece initially surprises us, almost all of its per-ceptual duration is involved with the fulfillment of expectancy. Although the effect is naturally more pronounced when many of Breer's small styrofoam floor pieces are seen together—as in his 1965 and 1967 shows at the Bonino Gallery where each work became merely part of a gallery-sized piece—even one of them has the ability to surprise through the denial and contradiction of the expectancies it creates. Unprepossessing in shape, devoid of detail, and painted a white that adds nothing to the visual interest, the piece hardly seems to move: in some of them, unseen wheels propel them so slowly that they do not appear to be in motion at all. The viewer is led to expect nothing and shifts his attention elsewhere. When he looks at the piece again, the object which appeared to be motionless is in a different spot; the piece traveling at a very slow rate has covered much more of the floor than was ex-pected, and perhaps it has even changed direction (a mech-anism inside reverses the wheels when the piece pushes against something). These effects depend primarily upon the fact that perceptual time tends to be judged according to the activity that fills it: an "empty" time seems long, a "busy" time seems short, etc. Of course no surprises occur with Breer's work if the piece is watched continually (in the "traditional" way) and no "different" time is interposed, but much of its aesthetic power lies in its ability to create no expectancies, to ingratiate itself into a life situation, and to provide what is not expected.

It should be apparent that in discussing the memory/expectancy mode of perception, I am referring only to those memories and expectancies which give a particular "shape" to time. Of course any piece of kinetic sculpture creates basic and obvious expectancies (and memories) as to location, material, qualities, etc. We know very quickly that Chryssa's piece will not move, that Breer's pieces will not change color or light up, etc. These expectancies relating to the general nature of the piece are qualitative and formal rather than structural. They give the piece its over-all character rather than its durational uniqueness. (Just as Beethoven, and others, could write many works in the symphonic form, Thomas Wilfred, and others, can make lumia which are formally the same but structurally different.) In other words the memory/expectancy qualities that involve structure rather than form are, or become, dynamic. The memory of a quality is passive while that of an occurrence tends to be active. An expectancy that is denied becomes a structural element, while an expectancy must have a degree of uncertainty before it can structure the future, etc. In short, while the numerous psychological principles involving the dynamics of memory and expectancy can not be investigated here, it can be said that every work exists in time, but not every work structures it. In this sense I believe that memory/expectancy is the only mode of perception in which we may say that a true structuring of time is involved. It is the mode most commonly operative in the traditional durational arts of music, drama, dance, etc., but it is not used in most kinetic sculpture. Although the other modes of kinetic experience partake of time, the same kind of "shape" through extended time is not realized.

If memory/expectancy is basically involved with time, we

can find a type of experience of kinetics that, in contrast, stands almost outside of time. It could be called the static mode.

In December, 1966, at the Pace Gallery, two visitors were discussing Marjorie Strider's *Piece of Sea*. Bending over the blocky green polyester shape, the upper face of which was modeled to resemble ocean waves, they peered closely at the rivulets of water that lined the surface. One proposed that— in contradiction to the law of gravity, for the surface obviously sloped—the water was not moving. The other agreed—until it was demonstrated to them that the water could be diverted and change direction.

In Strider's piece, streams of water flow from small holes in the highest part, run slowly and smoothly down the face and sides, and are recirculated from an almost invisible reservoir in the base. Light glints and shimmers from the surface of the water, but in many spots it is not easy to discern physical movement. This is not crucial to my point, however. Even when movement is easily apparent, there is no *change* in the movement. There is no point in comparing an observation at one moment with an observation at another moment. Memory and expectancy do not function dynamically. The piece is static. (Each time *Piece of Sea* is plugged in, the water takes a slightly different path. These "compositional" differences also do not matter. The piece is essentially unchanged.)

Thus in a static mode, kinesis creates a perceptual image that is not significantly different from a painted or sculpted one, although the quality of motion usually contributes a small share to the total experience. Static image sculpture of an entirely different sort than Strider's piece is the "virtual volume" work produced by the Bauhaus, Len Lye, etc.: a wire, plane, or solid of any kind is spun or rotated so rapidly that the observer sees a transparent and strangely immaterial "mass." Again movement is apparent. It is a quality of the image. But the image does not change with time. Memory/ expectancy is not utilized, and a photograph, which registers the quality of motion, represents the experience with relative accuracy. (The exclusion of memory/expectancy would not be possible, perhaps, if a comparison of the "on" and "off" states of the work was made an aesthetic consideration, but the purpose here is to establish general concepts rather than to analyze any particular work in detail.)

The question "How long is the present moment?" is crucial for another mode in the experience of kinesis. Theoretically the present may be infinitely small or have no real duration. But in actuality the *feeling* of presence has some extension in time. Practically and operationally we can consider the present to have a certain shape and size. These functional limits of the present are indicated by two basic psychological experiments.

In the first experiment, the experimenter briefly shows the subject a number of marbles in a box or a number of dots on a card, etc. The duration of exposure is not long enough to allow the subject to *count* the number of units shown him, but he is asked to tell how many there are. Not surprisingly, answers are accurate in the low numbers and decrease in accuracy as the total of marbles, dots, or whatever, increases. The number of items which the subject can estimate correctly without counting is known as the "apprehension span": it is usually about four to six units, depending upon the type of unit, if no errors are allowed. With larger numbers the subject usually will not even attempt any kind of specific response, saying "There are about thirty-five," etc.

The second experiment is immediate digit memory, which is a part of most intelligence tests. Number sequences of increasing length are presented to the subject, and, with no delay between presentation and response, he is asked to repeat them accurately. The average college student can usually repeat sequences up to eight digits.

These two experiments can be seen as representing the amplitude and duration, so to speak, of the present moment. A "vertical" limit on the simultaneous amount of material apprehended is indicated by the former experiment, and a "horizontal" limit on continuity and sequence is emphasized by the latter. [Within these limits a certain type of memory and expectancy probably exist, but I prefer to use those terms for connections across "empty" intervals of the past and future. Rather than differentiating between "continuous" and "discontinuous" memory, for example, it is best to use the word "memory" only as we have previously and to stress the wholistic character of the present moment.]

Since the present moment has a certain amplitude, the experience of a kinetic work may exist entirely within its limits and yet not, of necessity, be static. In contrast to the static mode, it develops and changes. In contrast to the memory/ expectancy mode, it is perceived totally without any extended dynamic claims to the past or future. Thus *Bascule* by Jean Tinguely, for example, rocks back and forth on a large curved metal plate while the belt-drive from its visible and organic motor turns a wheel which thrusts a bell-tipped metal rod out into space. Where in the static mode we had an image with the quality of motion, we now have a complete, sequential motion image that makes no claims on memory or expectation.

By referring to the concepts of memory/expectancy and of the present moment, we find that another mode of perception exists somewhat between the two. Naturally, as the perceptions of the present moment move into the past, they disappear: the complete, wholistic present can be "stretched" only so far. This disappearance is accelerated if new stimuli are presented rather than a neutral sensory field. In some cases, of course, elements of the present moment function as memories and create expectancies in the manner already discussed, but the point is that this creation of significant, functional memory does not necessarily happen. No matter how interesting the details of the present moment are, they may be completely unavailable to memory in a very short time.

Thus we have what perhaps could be called the "transitional mode" of kinetic perception, in which a series of different present moments flow one into the other without creating operative memories or expectancies.

In the lumia works of Thomas Wilfred and his imitators,

light is reflected onto the rear of a translucent screen, creating an abstract "painting" that is constantly changing. During each present moment we are aware of the type and direction of changes in color and form; of the character of the appearing, expanding, contracting, disappearing shapes; of the tempo or "pace" of the composition. A comparison might be made between a new image and one that has just faded away, but, as in digit memory, the mind can only hold the complete details of the sequence for a short time. It is not the aesthetic purpose of most lumia to implant their complete sequence in memory. (A Museum of Modern Art press release of 1964 describing the newly acquired *Lumia Suite. Op. 158* states, "The duration of the entire composition has not yet been calculated, but the length of other lumia compositions by Wilfred ranges from a few hours to more than 5,000 years.") Whether the imagery itself actually flows or is presented as a series of motionless configurations, etc., we have in the transitional mode a flow of present moments that do not attempt to hook up with the past or future.

In using lumia as our example, we must note that the form is not necessarily involved with the transitional mode. If we are told or assume that the structure is cyclical, expectancy may be operative as we search for the repetitions. If a form or color cycle is short, we may recognize it when it begins for the second or third time. With longer cycles, however, it is problematical how many repetitions would be necessary before memory/expectancy became involved, and since "beginning" and "end" are arbitrary, the usual mode involves a "wash" of various present moments which totally replace each other.

Although Harold Rosenberg (in *Vogue,* February 1, 1967) states that the contemporary aesthetic concern with motion "marks the end of contemplation," the transitional mode in particular can be seen as a contemplative one. As illustrated by Wilfred's lumia (or by "psychedelic" light shows) the ever changing present contains too much detail to be completely apprehended, and past and future cease to exist: the "timelessness" of traditional contemplation is obtained in a different way. And since, on the other hand, the static mode is as "present" as a painting and no details are added or taken away by time, its contemplative possibilities would not seem to differ from the traditional ones.

Thus we have four modes in the perception of kinetic sculpture: the static, the present moment (or motion image), the transitional, and memory/expectancy. The important thing is that each is fundamentally unlike the others. Each has its own psychic territory, its own way of functioning. Investigation of the subtleties and nuances of these modes can only tell us more about art in general, because, in a very basic way, the experience is the work of art.